BEING AND LOGOS

BEING AND LOGOS

Categorical and Generic Analyses of Being in Classical Philosophy

edited by
Agnieszka Woszczyk
and
Dariusz Olesiński

Kraków – Katowice 2012

Reviewer:
dr hab. Dorota Zygmuntowicz

Proofread:
Editorial Staff

Cover design:
Anna M. Damasiewicz

Picture on the cover:
© *Antonio Abrignani | Depositphotos.com*

Desktop publisher:
Alicja Kuźma

Publication was funded by the University of Silesia in Katowice

ISBN 978-83-7850-146-6

Oficyna Wydawnicza "Impuls"
30-619 Kraków, ul. Turniejowa 59/5
tel./fax: (12) 422 41 80, 422 59 47, 506 624 220
www.impulsoficyna.com.pl, e-mail: impuls@impulsoficyna.com.pl
Edition I, Kraków 2012

Contents

Introduction

Since the beginning of history of philosophy, the specificity of philosophical knowledge, which results from its fundamentality, has manifested itself in the quest for the most general notions which would adequately describe the structure and dynamics of reality. Such notions as oneness and multiplicity, sameness and difference, finitude and infinity, changeability and unchangeability, motion and rest, among others, have become a permanent challenge for philosophizing intellect, and also an irremovable element of the dictionary of European philosophy, to which new terminological entries are being added, and the meanings of the old ones are being specified.

From the very beginning, their fundamental understanding has been disputed, namely, it has been argued whether they result from a subjective description of the world, or they reflect and name objective manners of being. Consequently, there have occurred epistemological and linguistic interpretations (categories as notions or predicates), and ontological interpretations (categories as ideas or various substantial forms.)

This monograph is devoted to the analysis of different meanings of these generic and categorical notions which occurred in the history of classical philosophy, as well as relations between them. In the first presented text "Archelaus: Between Ontology and Anthropology" Adam Drozdek analyzes how the meaning of the main category of Anaxagoras' ontology, i.e. the cosmic Mind, is modified in the philosophy of Archelaus. On the one hand, Archelaus decreased the elevated status of the cosmic Mind by allowing it to be mixed with other beings, on the other hand, he made a human soul to be a part of the Mind, thereby elevating the status of man, and introducing the anthropological perspective, which was absent in Anaxagoras' philosophy.

Then, in the perspective of a general reflection on basic understandings of categories which occurred in the philosophical tradition, in his "Categories in the Philosophy of Plato and Aristotle" Bogdan Dembiński characterizes similarities and differences between those two most important ancient viewpoints, namely, those of Plato and Aristotle. A category introduced by Aristotle turned out to be a direct reference to Plato's thinking, especially to the conception of the most superior kinds presented in *The Sophist*. However, this notion was linked by Aristotle with basic manners of substantial being, as well as, linguistically, with the basic forms of predication on being. Dariusz Olesiński ("Plato's Conception of the Good in *The Republic*") also refers to the Platonic tradition, and he focuses on the meaning of the good in Plato's philosophy. As it is justified by the author, the twofold nature of the good, i.e. the absolute and relative one, which is singled out in Book II of *The Republic,* turns out to be crucial for the understanding of Plato's characteristics of the Good from the central part of the dialogue, depicted especially by employing the analogy of the sun. Consequently, the supremacy of the Good over other ideas (its status of ἐπέκεινα τῆς οὐσίας) does not mean absolute transcendence of being but is the expression of its power, adequately presented by the category of an ultimate cause (αἰτία) of reality.

On the other hand, Anna Zhyrkova in "The Academic Roots of Plotinus' Treatment of the Aristotelian Categories" reconstructs the Academic and Middle Platonic interpretation of the Aristotelian categories, and she criticizes a common belief according to which the standpoint of Plotinus seems contrary to the Middle Platonic one. Therefore, the author argues that both Plotinus and his Neo-platonic successors created their conceptions based on the same Platonic tradition of interpreting Aristotle's categories, which was historically rooted a few centuries ago. Then in "The Highest Genera of Being and Substantial Unity in Plotinus' Ontology" Rafał Oleś outlines Plotinus' generic analysis of being, focusing on the explanation of the nature of interdependence and oneness of the most superior kinds (being, motion, rest, sameness and difference) both, for the corporal substance (the analysis of the nature of body and soul), and for the noetic substance (the analysis of formal attributes of the most superior kinds). In the subsequent text on Plotinian thinking ("Prenoetic Genera in *The Enneads* by Plotinus"), Agnieszka Woszczyk points at the necessity of distinguishing between two perspectives in Plotinus' presentation of principal kinds (μέγιστα γένη), firstly, the immanent analysis of being which leads to an understanding of kinds in the context of noetic world; secondly, the genetic analysis of being which involves referring it (as the noetic unity of multiplicity) to transcendental principles of the One and Indefinite Dyad. In the latter perspective, the kinds are what precedes and facilitates the analysis of being, and hence obtains the pre-noetic status.

The monograph ends with "Disjunctives as Transcategorial Attributes of Being – An Outline of John Duns Scotus's Standpoint" by Jacek Surzyn, however, at the same time this text opens the perspective for reflection on the importance of the development of a categorical and generic analysis of being in the Middle Ages. The author considers in detail the opinion which John Duns Scotus represented in the discussion on the disjunction as one of the aspects of understanding transcategorial properties of being (e.g., absolute-relative, infinite-finite, substance-accident, cause-effect). The author shows that Scotus' original understanding of disjunction can be interpreted as an important bridge between the ancient Aristotelian tradition of conceiving categories and their modern Kantian conception.

Certainly, this monograph is not an exhaustive presentation of this subject since it is impossible to present it exhaustively when we remember that generic and categorical classifications of being represent the pivotal issue of the whole philosophical tradition, at least the classically conceived tradition. However, taking into consideration unquestionable importance of this issue as well as its complexity, even a modest contribution to the elucidation of here addressed questions seems needed, and the effort of addressing them appears justified. The authors of this volume, which is now being offered to the Reader, also believe that such a contribution is valuable.

Agnieszka Woszczyk
Dariusz Olesiński

Adam Drozdek

Archelaus: Between Ontology and Anthropology

ABSTRACT: Archelaus simplified Anaxagoras' ontology by rejecting the everything in everything principle and reduced the elevated status of cosmic Mind by allowing it to be mixed with other beings. Also, he made the soul to be a fragment of Mind, thereby elevating the status of humans over other animate and inanimate beings. This led to Archelaus' interest in anthropological and social issues, which is almost nonexistent in Anaxagorean fragments, and he passed this concern with human affairs to Socrates.

A vexing problem in ancient philosophy was that nothing comes from nothing. There are a variety of ways to address the problem. One possibility is that nothing *comes* from nothing: since there is no motion, no coming to be, no emergence of new entities. The world is altogether static, there is no change, everything simply exists. This is a solution proposed by Parmenides. Another solution is that there is a primary source of everything that exists and everything comes from this one source: water (Thales), the *apeiron* which is infinity in pure form (Anaximander), air (Anaximenes, Diogenes), and fire (Heraclitus). Everything is just a manifestation of one particular substance. Sometimes, there may be a certain number of sources, like the two original substances proposed by Xenophanes or four substances used by Empedocles. However, even singling out one substance (or multiple substances) as the origin leaves room for too much novelty and paradoxical connections. If air is the original substance, then stone, metal, and diamond are but forms of existence of air, which may be stretching the credibility of such a solution too much. Also, it can be claimed that something does come from nothing, after all; otherwise, how can the hardness of stone come from the softness of air? This may have been Anaxagoras' train of reasoning when he proposed that all substances, homoiomeries (cf. 59B10), exist from eternity, and paradoxically, every substance exists in every other substance, to solve, for instance, the problem of nourishment: there is already bone, muscle, etc., in an olive, so that eating the olive can fortify the body and contribute to the growth of various tissues. Otherwise, how could such a phenomenon be explained? Actually, Democritus could have claimed that his atomism provided such explanation fairly easily.

The existence of homoiomeries directly addresses the problem of nothing coming from nothing, but it is insufficient to explain the orderliness of the world. Therefore, a seat of rationality in the universe was needed. Some Presocratics blended together rationality with the original substance; some of them found a separate seat. And so did Anaxagoras by positing a cosmic and eternal Mind, unmixed with anything else and yet responsible for the order of the universe by setting it into motion, whereby an infinity of worlds came into being. By being unmixed, Mind presumably could retain its rationality in undisturbed form and thereby inject orderliness into the universe and its infinity of worlds which are not unlike the earth.

At the beginning of Anaxagoras' universe, there existed the opposites, homoiomerous elements, in particular, the four basic Empedoclean elements, and finally seeds. This mixture was brought into motion by Mind that exists in separation from everything else, mixed with no other entity. Therefore, in the primal mixture there were all possible substances as well as a modicum of organization in the form of seeds from which mature beings sprang after Mind activated their potentiality. Anaxagoras also introduced the everything in everything principle (EEP), one of the most interesting ontological principles conceived in ancient thought: substances never exist in pure form; if they are divided into smaller and smaller parts, then eventually everything else can be encountered.[1] For instance, when water divides into smaller and smaller parts, fire, earth, and also bone, muscles, etc. can be found. If these particles are further divided, then fire, earth, and also bone, muscles, etc. can be found, etc. into infinity. In today's terminology, the principle can be explained by considering each entity as a fractal that resembles itself regardless of the level of its division.

Sources state that Archelaus "spoke of a mixture of matter similarly as Anaxagoras and of first principles" (Hippolytus, *Ref.* 1.9.1-6 = 60A4.1), and further description mentions only the hot, the cold, and three Empedoclean elements: water, earth, and air (the fourth element, fire, is mentioned in Diogenes Laertius 2.17 = A1.17 and Sextus Empiricus 9.360 = = A7);

> [...] he gives the same first principles as Anaxagoras. They say that the first principles are infinite in number and different in kind, and they set homoiomeries as principles (Simplicius, *In Phys*. 27.26-28 = A5);

---

[1] A. Drozdek, *Anaxagoras and the Everything in Everything Principle*, "Hermes" 2005, 133, pp. 163–177.

> Archelaus thought that all [things] consist of particles similar to one another out of which all particular [things] are made (Augustine, *De civ. Dei* 8.2 = A10).

In all three accounts, homoiomeries are only briefly mentioned assuming that "particles similar to one another" is a circumlocution referring to them.[2] Another possibility would be seeds, but seeds are certainly not similar to one another (cf. 59B4a). Also, seeds are contained in everything through the EEP, but homoiomeries constitute the main mass of each being. Thus, Archelaus apparently modified the system by disposing of seeds so that the primal mass was truly disorganized, which raises the problem of the origin of order in the created world. Moreover, Archelaus does not appear to have retained the EEP: because of the paradoxical nature of this principle, it is unlikely that the doxographers would not have mentioned it, had Archelaus kept it in his system. Thus, the primal mass is a mixture of an infinite number of primal substances – homoiomeries – and opposites. However, there seems to be some redundancy in this ontological setup. For example, in his cosmogony,

> [...] the origin of motion is the separation of the hot and the cold from one another: the hot moves, the cold is at rest. Melted water flows to the middle where it burns and becomes (γίνεσθαι) air and earth, of which the former goes upwards, the latter remains below (60A4.2; A1.17).

According to this report, water *becomes* air and earth, an argument that approximates Thales' rather than Anaxagoras' reasoning. The latter spoke about separation – e.g., the dense is separated off from the rare (B12), earth separated off from water (B16, cf. B13, B14) – although separation is never perfect on account of the EEP. In this way, it appears that for Archelaus – true to the spirit of the Ionians – one substance would be sufficient as the primary source of other substances and Mind would have used proper motion to generate other substances. Positing an infinity of

[2] Anaxagoras and Archelaus believed that infinitely numerous particles are not atoms but homoiomeries, according to Alexander, *De mixtione* 214.1-3 and Simplicius, *In De caelo* 604.3032.

substances would be required if turning one substance into another would be irreversible – getting air and earth from water would be possible, but not vice versa – or only limited kinds of substances could be generated from other substances. It appears, however, that Archelaus' system was interpreted in the Ionian manner, since it was believed that for him the first principle and element of all is air (A7); that the first principle is "infinite air with all things condensed and rarefied in it, of the former being fire, of the latter – water" (Aetius 1.3.6 = A7); that "hot and cold are principles of all" (Hermias, *Irrisio* 11 = A8, A1.16); and that "everything came into being from earth since it is the principle of all" (A9). These reports disagree about what exactly the first principles were and perhaps Archelaus was not too specific about it himself. He allowed for some substances to be converted into other substances, but if he really allowed for infinity of substances in the primal mixture, it was not obvious, what substances could become origination points for other substances. But maybe some qualifications need to be added to see some consistency in this variety of first principles. The hot and the cold could be first cosmic principles since separation of one from another marks the beginning of cosmogony (A4.2). Air could be considered the first principle in the sense that all celestial bodies (except for the earth) originated from it (A4.3). Finally, earth could be taken as the first principle of life:

> [...] about animals he says that when, at first, the earth grew hot in the lower part where the hot and the cold were mixed, many other animals appeared, and humans, all having the same mode of life, feeding from the mud (these [animals] were short-lived), but later they were born from one another (A4.5).[3]

What is the cosmic role of Mind? Archelaus believed, like Anaxagoras, that the cosmos was created at a certain time after motion began, initiated by Mind; before that, all things were static (Simplicius, *In Phys.* 1121.23-24 = 59A64). However, in respect to the organization of the

[3] "There is no doubt that this doctrine of Archelaus presupposes the [traditional] belief in Mother Earth", V. Tilman, *Archélaos d'Athènes*, "Revue de philosophie ancienne" 2000, 18, p. 88.

world, the role of Mind is vastly different in their systems. Archelaus is said to have called "air and Mind the God, but the Mind was not cosmos-making (κοσμοποίος)" (Aetius 1.7.14 = A12), whereas Anaxagoras called Mind *kosmopoios* (Simplicius, *In Phys.* 1123.23 = 59A45, Aetius 1.7.5 = = A48). It appears that Archelaus' Mind did not create a world, that is, did not turn disorganized masses into an organized world, the cosmos. Mind is responsible only for motion in the universe since "everything is moved by Mind" (Philoponus, *De anima* 71.17 = A18). It is a seat of energy radiating into the homoiomerous masses, thereby releasing their self-organizing potentials. Mind seems to be only a principle of motion, but not the principle of orderliness, at least not on the cosmic scale.[4] This orderliness seems to be built into the nature of primal substances: Mind provides the first impulse and then maintains the motion of cosmic substances, but they organize themselves into particular entities and other substances due to their nature and to the mechanism of separation and rarefaction.

Archelaus' Mind does not maintain an elevated status of separation as does Anaxagoras', but is blended with matter: "from the beginning [there was] a certain mixture in Mind" (60A4.1). In this way, Mind has intimate contact with matter and, presumably, can influence it more effectively than if it were mixed with nothing. Mind acts on all eternal bodies, that is, all particles that are similar to one another, bringing them together and pushing them apart. These particles, that is, homoiomeries can then organize into meaningful wholes.

Like Anaxagoras, Archelaus believed that an infinity of worlds exist in the universe (Aetius 2.1.3 = A13) and that Mind controls infinities, that is, all these infinite worlds (Clement, *Protr.* 5.66 = A11). Control-

[4] This also seems to be the meaning of an interpretation which states that "Mind is not creator of the cosmos" is related to the assumption that "the details of his cosmogony were explained in mechanistic terms even more than in Anaxagoras", G. Betegh, *The Derveni Papyrus: Cosmology, Theology and Interpretation*, Cambridge 2004, p. 322. The denial of "the title of cosmopoeic" indicated that "Archelaus seems to have been even more open than Anaxagoras to the charge of leaving the making of the universe to the causal interplay of mechanical natural forces", W.K.C. Guthrie, *A History of Greek Philosophy*, Cambridge 1965, vol. 2, p. 341; cf. 59A47.

ling these worlds may mean that Mind is just a source of their motion. However, since Mind is called the God, it would be difficult to think about it as simply a seat of unintelligible energy. Mind appears to have some organizational influence on these worlds, after all. It seems to leave the organization of prime homoiomerous substances into worlds to the organizing potentials of these substances. However, when the worlds arise, then Mind seems to exercise direct influence on their affairs. On the micro level – on the level of particular beings – the organizing potentials of substances are insufficient to bring particular beings into existence, the influence of a divine intelligence is necessary to make this happen. Because intelligibility hardly resided in an inanimate entity, Mind can be considered to be alive and, possibly, even the source and principle of life. In this way, the statement that "the cosmos arose from the hot and aliveness (ἐμψυχία)" (Aetius 2.4.5 = A14) can be taken to mean that the hot was a principal factor in organizing matter into a cosmos – cf. the statement that "the origin of motion is the separation of the hot and the cold from one another" (A4.2) – but life in the cosmos itself results from the controlling influence of Mind.

Anaxagoras spoke about Mind that it is mixed with nothing, but he also stated that Mind is present in some things (59B11), which seem to be living beings since Mind controls everything with a soul (B12). That is, Mind is present in living beings, but not mixed with them. This seems necessary to account for the intelligibility of ensouled beings: the soul is a principle of life, but not of intelligibility, so rationality of such beings is really rationality of Mind: Mind thinks through them.[5] Anaxagoras recognized different levels of intelligence in living beings (Aristotle, *De anima* 404b4-6 = A100) – and these intelligent living beings even included plants (Plutarch, *Quaest. phys.* 911d = A116), though he considered humans to be most intelligent (Aristotle, *De part. an.* 687a8-9 = A102). Archelaus seems to have agreed with this when he said that

[5] A. Drozdek, *Anaxagoras and Human Rationality*, "Archiwum Historii Filozofii i Myśli Społecznej" 2010, 55, pp. 27–35.

> Mind is inborn in all animals alike; for each of the animals uses the mind/Mind, some more slowly, others more quickly (60A4.6);

that is, there are clearly different levels of intelligibility among living beings, and it is possible that Archelaus also ascribed its highest level to humans. He is slightly more specific about Mind's presence in living beings: it is in them from the very beginning of their existence. Because Archelaus allowed for Mind to be mixed with other entities, Mind can be mixed into living beings. Its elevated position is further diminished by the fact that Mind is used by a living being and hence Mind is, to some extent, under the control of that being. When he said that a being "uses the mind/Mind", it may be taken to mean that this being uses its own mind as though this individual mind were a portion of the cosmic Mind, something spawned from it, or maybe a portion of Mind that for the lifetime of that being is allotted to this being's use; a portion of Mind on loan, as it were. This is possible since, according to Archelaus, the soul is like air (ἀερώδη, 60A17; Theodoret 5.18). At the same time, as mentioned, he called "air and Mind the God" (A12), that is, apparently he identified Mind and air, thereby bringing his theory close to that of Anaximenes and of his contemporary Diogenes of Apollonia. Moreover, "motion [belongs] to the soul" (A18), and Mind is a cosmic principle of motion, whereby an individual soul would appear to be a fragment splintered off from Mind. In this way, the soul would be a portion of the divine Mind, thereby possessing a measure of sacredness. For Anaxagoras, the soul was not a fragment of Mind. Mind was in the soul to control it and exercise its rationality through it, but the soul itself was not rational.

Archelaus "tries to bring something of his own in the genesis of cosmos and other [subjects]" (A5), and he did contribute something different from Anaxagoras. Archelaus' ontology is arguably inferior to that of his teacher because Archelaus apparently rejected the EEP and, as it were, flattened the hierarchy of existence. Anaxagoras' infinite hierarchy – in everything can be found everything, regardless of how far the division of entities goes – there are only two levels: substances (homoiomeries and opposites) and particular beings composed of these substances. Also, the elevated status of Mind is reduced by renouncing its unmixed existence. Mind becomes immanent in nature by being mixed with it and being an intricate part of it since it appears to be one of the substances, air, which is the most tenuous substance and thus the closest to the immaterial substance of Anaxagoras' Mind.[6] What Anaximenes did to Anaximander's lofty ontological vision, Archelaus did to Anaxagoras' by making it more acceptable to common sense.[7] However, the status of the human being in Anaxagoras' system is not quite enviable since it does not even have its own rationality. By making the soul a fragment of Mind, Mind in miniature, Archelaus truly elevated the status of humans over other animate and inanimate beings. Humans, as it were, stand on their own feet by becoming Mind on a human scale, not truly gods, since mortality is not abolished (after all, the worlds are perishable (A14), and thus humans in them) – but having significantly more dignified status than in the Anaxagorean universe. This led to Archelaus' interest in human affairs, which is almost nonexistent in Anaxagorean fragments. In this way, Archelaus did not simply diminish Anaxagorean ontology, but, in a way, he transferred part of its loftiness into philosophical anthropology. The elevated status of Mind was sacrificed to raise the status of humans so that, philosophically, their position in the world was improved. This was very much in the spirit of the times.[8]

Early Presocratics were interested primarily in ontology and metaphysics. However, with the sophists and, most forcefully, with Socrates, interest shifted toward human affairs and the position of man in the universe and society, which led to discussions of origin and structure of society – real

---

[6] "Without a doubt, he wanted to designate something that would simultaneously resemble the material (the seeds of matter) and the quasi-material (Mind)", V. Tilman, *op. cit.*, p. 83. Translations of all fragments in this article come from the author.

[7] "He had a firm desire to hold on to facts – the way he understood them, to never go beyond them, but only explain the unknown by means of what humans already know from experience, *a posteriori*", C. Périphanakis, *Quelques traits de la philosophie sociale d'Archélaos d'Athenès (Ve siècle av. J.-C.)*, Athènes 1951, p. 7.

[8] "The 'sophistic' and Attic interest for the more pressing problem of human society was for [Archelaus] more important than the investigation of the μετήορα. Therefore, the region of 'heaven' was for him the one from which stemmed the soul [made out] of aethereal matter", F. Lämmli, *Vom Chaos zum Kosmos*, Basel 1962, vol. 2, p. 189, note 757.

and ideal, an interest in the nature of ethics and laws. In this way, a persistently repeated claim that Archelaus was a teacher of Socrates (A2; SE 9.360 = A7; DL 10.12 = 59A26; Augustine, *De civ. Dei* 8.2) should not be easily dismissed even if Plato and Aristotle did not mention Archelaus.[9] He was not an insignificant personality of his times; indeed, Theophrastus wrote a book about him (DL 5.43 = before A4) and claims were made that the school in Lampsacus which Archelaus first took over from Anaxagoras (Eusebius, *Praep. ev.* 10.14, 14.14) was in turn taken over by Socrates (Theodoret, *Graec. aff. cur.* 2.22). Perhaps Archelaus was not a teacher in the full meaning of the word and Socrates only associated with him (A5, A3) or listened to his lectures (DL 2.19 = Nachtrag 60; Clement, *Strom.* 1.63.3), but the claim that he influenced Socrates in ethical matters (A1.16) is very credible. If this is the case, Archelaus would have been a thinker who, although interested in ontology, did not make it his primary area of philosophical interest, but who was equally interested in anthropological and social issues influencing Socrates with the latter interest to the extent that Socrates abandoned his studies of natural philosophy and concentrated on ethics. Plato restored philosophical balance creating a grand ontological system and the equally impressive social system of Callipolis and Magnesia and by showing that ontology does have social

[9] "The teacher-pupil relationship between Archelaus and Socrates ... is a doxographic construction of the school of Aristotle in the fourth century", claimed L. Woodbury, *Socrates and Archelaus*, "Phoenix" 1971, 25, p. 309. However, as to Plato's silence, "one may guess that precisely this [teacher-pupil] affinity has something to do with Plato's attitude, respectfully inherited by Aristotle", D. Panchenko, *The Shape of the Earth in Archelaus, Democritus and Leucippus*, "Hyperboreus" 1999, 5, p. 22. Also, Plato and Aristotle "had good reasons for passing over lightly the earlier materialistic and democratic associations of Socrates", A.D. Winspear, T. Silverberg, *Who Was Socrates?*, New York 1960, p. 37. It may be that Plato did not mention Archelaus since he concentrated on atomism, "materialism in the strongest form", and concern about Archelaus' views took back seat, F. Lämmli, *op. cit.*, p. 179, note 721; "apparently, purposely and with success [Archelaus] was passed with silence" by Plato, A. Rüstow, *Ortsbestimmung der Gegenwart*, Erlenbach-Zürich 1952, vol. 2, p. 541. Mean-spirited stories of Aristoxenus about Socrates, including his relation between Archelaus and Socrates (frs. 52, 54–59, Wehrli) are very unreliable, but they would make no sense "and would be without weight if an association between Socrates and Archelaus was not largely recognized", V. Tilman, *op. cit.*, p. 71.

relevance and that social and ethical investigation cannot be conducted in total separation from ontological issues. In this general approach, Plato reverted to the philosophical attitude championed by Archelaus and, if in nothing else, Archelaus proves to be an important figure in the history of philosophy.

Bogdan Dembiński

Categories in the Philosophy of Plato and Aristotle

ABSTRACT: This is a discussion about general characteristics of Plato's and Aristotle's standpoints, since it can be assumed that they were the most important ones for ancient thinking. Plato was accused of treating an idea as an hypostatized notion. An idea is not a notion but its expressed by a notion. Certainly, this notion is a general one, it is a manner of articulating an idea. However, this cannot mean that an idea itself is a notion, or a hypostatized notion. Since no notion can be a cause of being, and existential predication of any actual state of affairs.

The term *category* has many meanings in Greek philosophy. First of all, derived from the colloquial language, it was bound up with the legal domain where it meant an indictment formulated in prosecutors' speeches.[1] Soon however, it became associated with various contexts of predicating forms of determinate states of things. Undoubtedly for this reason, it was referred to grammatical structures of the language, most of all. It may be conjectured that the notion of category comprised the highest genera determining the distinguished states of things. Such dealings already had a long tradition. Greek philosophers assumed that states of the world should be described by means of tolerably general notions, which express basic manners wherein their existence is determined. They appear at the very inception of philosophy and they are directly related to the issues of cognition and possibility of articulating its results. Philosophers discerned the specific property of cognition which is manifested in describing the world and its states by means of such notions as: oneness and multiplicity, identity and differentiation, limit and limitlessness, variability and invariability, movement and rest, part and whole. One may mention more of such genera. They constitute naming the states which predicate of everything which is existent in any way. They may also be defined as notions comprising common features of different things and states of things. From the very beginning the dispute on their comprehension was going on. It was considered whether they constitute merely the consequence of the subjective way of describing the world or they are the reflection and naming of ways of being, independent of the subjective determination. It may be suspected that it was related to generality which appeared in these notions, whose sources were perceived either in the nature of language and intellect or the nature of the world. It had a direct influence on the interpretation of those notions. There were logico-linguistic interpretations (predicates) and ontological interpretations (ideas, substantial forms). These conceptions were crowned in the medieval dispute over universalia.

[1] See Arystoteles, *Kategorie*, trans. by K. Leśniak. The translator's preface, p. 26. Warszawa 1990.

In my deliberations I would like to undertake the general characterization of two stances represented by Plato and Aristotle. For it may be acknowledged that they were the most significant for ancient thought.

The first stance, a Platonic one, emerges directly from Socratic intuitions. Socrates in his philosophical dealings perceived the essence of knowledge in formulating precise definitions, which created on the basis of induction, grasp the essence of things which may be expressed by means of a general notion. To reach the essence of things means: to find (in the definition) the right meaning of a general notion (e.g. Beauty, Goodness or Valour) which expresses that essence. It was the basis of conviction (later adopted by Plato and Aristotle) that knowledge refers to something which is general and related solely to something which is general. Socrates was looking for correct definitions, whereas he connected the skill of formulating them with the intellectual competence of the person who managed to present such a definition. Aristotle speaks about it:

> […] two findings may be fairly ascribed to Socrates: inductive reasoning and universal definition, for one and the other concern the beginning of knowledge.[2] […]
>
> Socrates however, [not] being interested in the nature of the world as a whole, dealt with ethical problems, searching for general notions among them and for the first time directed his attention to definitions.[3]

It may be legitimately claimed that the essence of general notion related to the essence of things, examined by Socrates, inclines to the question, necessary in this case, about the status of essence and the notion inherent in it. It concerns such notions as Beauty, Goodness, Justice, Valour, Piety, etc. What do these notions correspond with? Socrates, while using intuitively the induction method, becomes convinced that (contrary to the Sophists' stance) they are not an optional formation of the subject. He holds that those notions are "elicited" in the process of abstract thinking from the actual states of things. For instance, the notion of justice is the result of inductive

---

[2] Arystoteles, *Metafizyka*, trans. by K. Leśniak, Warszawa 1983, 1078b.
[3] *Ibidem*, 987b.

process of analysis of the actual deeds denominated by Greeks as just. What is collective in these deeds becomes separated by the power of abstraction from what is unitary (actual persons, circumstances, characteristic to those deeds) and introduced within the definition. The general definition of justice built this way is the one, by means of which an attempt is made to express the essence of justice, thus the collective property inherent in actual just deeds. Naturally the question appears: What are the essences which are the content of Socratic definitions? How does the essence of justice differ from the actual just deed? How does valour differ from its actual cases? It should also be asked: What is the status of the notion which expresses this essence? They are problems which Socrates did not yet manage to raise and develop. It was later accomplished by Plato and his followers.

It should be admitted that Plato was fully aware of the difficulties which appear as a result of asking questions of that kind. He became convinces that the essences which Socrates exhibits in his definitions indicate the existence of an autonomous domain, independent of spatiotemporal realizations and determination of the subject, which accounts for its ultimate substantiation. He noticed that the essences appearing in definitions (Justice, Beauty or Goodness), provided they are independent of subjective determination, they must have its ultimate ontic basis which itself makes them possible. He defined this basis and denominated it as idea.

He acknowledged that idea is something which makes the essence possible, grasped in a general notion and its definition. Thereby, idea appears as the ultimate substantiation of every essence. The thing is, that the essences which express the content and sense of actual states of things require substantiation themselves. The concrete just deeds, whose essence is expressed in a definition by means of a general notion, must obtain the substantiation of their existence and their determinacy. In Plato's view they are constituted each time by a proper idea, the measure of all just deeds. As far as there may be many just deeds and each of them has the proper essence, expressed in the definition, then the idea of justice may be only one. It is easy to present through the example of the idea of circle. As circles of any kind may be many, the measure of circularity must be only one. One cannot accept the existence of many measures of circularity. The essence of circle is expressed in the definition of circle and clearly results in the fact that the definition of circle is not and cannot be the same as the measure of any circularity. In this way essence distinguishes itself from idea. It entails frequent mistaking essence for idea by commentators. Certainly, idea is present in essence but idea is something more than essence, since essence is always the essence of an actual state of things (later remarked by Aristotle), contrary to idea which is always one, eternal and invariable. Idea, however, is not cognitively available to us in a direct way. It is always available by the essence which is grasped in the actual states of things. Concurrently, one should realize the fact that general notions which describe essences are each time formations of subject and depend absolutely on its presence. While applying an example from the domain of contemporary natural science we may say that it cannot be claimed that physical laws are the same as their definitions which express the essence of laws. They are not the same as their definitions either. Essences depend in their existence on neither the language of subject nor, in general, on its presence. Nevertheless, when as cognizing subjects we try to understand laws and the mode of their activity we must express them in some language, by means of definite notions. In case of physical laws the most precise language is the language of mathematics and notions characteristic of them. Therefore in these notions physical laws should be uttered.

Plato recognized that the essences revealed by Socrates in definitions, inherent in actual states of things, point out to the existence of an autonomous ontic domain which determines the existence and possibility to define essences themselves. It should be immediately taken into account that ideas cannot be understood as objects or quasi-objects whose presence and existence may be grasped as the presence of things in things. They do not have any temporal or spatial character, they constitute solely the determinacy measures of something which exists really or ideally. The term *ideally* requires a particular explanation. Now we are confronting a certain quandary. For if we speak about a physical law, ideas or mathematical subjects then we attribute an ideal existence to all these states. It is necessary to be cautious. Physical laws exist ideally, in the sense that they do not exist like things or phenomena which are their manifestation. In turn, they do not exist like mathematical subjects, irrespective of the fact whether we acknowledge an autonomous mode of existence of mathematical subjects or we maintain that mathematical subjects merely account for the result of intellectual activity of subject. In this sense we must claim that mathematical subjects also exist ideally, but it is immediately seen that their mode of existence is different from the mode of existence of physical laws. Aristotle pointed out this difficulty regarding that we are allowed to speak only about essences and we should not introduce an additional, independent existence of autonomous, supranoetic ideas. For how would ideas differ from essences? As separate ideas, in Aristotle's opinion, they cannot be the cause of concrete, unitary substances. There appears a trouble with determining the mode of existence of ideas and distinguishing them from the mode of existence of essences (substantial forms). We may fall into the regress of infinite substantiation of existence of successive ontic levels (apory of the third man). We might be at a loss here, accustomed to solely a narrow comprehension of ideality, since everything is "ideal alike", principles and laws, mathematical beings or products of the thought. Meanwhile Plato suggests their clear discrimination. He distinguishes ideas from mathematical subjects, and these in turn from products of thought and phenomena. The matter becomes even more complicated when in the late phase of his science Plato postulates the necessity of adoption of ontic principles (One and Indeterminate Dyad) situated over ideas and whose task is the explanation of multiplicity and differentiation of ideas. In that case it may be inferred that, just like we deal with many forms of spatiotemporal existence, we also deal with and might deal with many forms of ideal existence. Further, if we want to distinguish conceptually all domains of ideal existence we must properly use the concepts which may rightly articulate those domains. For one should take the highest precautions attributing specific notions to specific states of things. One should also analyse very precisely the relationships which occur between notions themselves. A mistake may lead to a fateful, improper comprehension of reality when not only do we confuse notions, but also we confuse the modes of existence of reality. Therefore, it is necessary to adopt the method which allows to use notions correctly, examines relationships which occur between them and examines references of notions to the structures which express a specific mode of existence. This method is the dialectic method. Its possibility results from the particular assumption adopted by Plato and his disciples. It is based on the conviction that our intellect, whose power makes us capable of describing reality, constitutes itself the form of this reality which it strives to describe. Thus, the notions proper to language are not solely optional products of the subject but in the essential part they represent realities which they are the product themselves, irrespective of the fact whether the reality is real or ideal. Certainly, we have the ability to create the notions which are not the manifestation of reality (mental beings) but it is an additional ability. Using the language and notions which are its ingredients we are capable, acting cautiously and methodologically, of describing properly the reality itself. The function of language understood this way results from the conviction that we possess the mode of cognition which Plato denominates as anamnesis.[4] Apparently, it does not refer to merely a mythical image of ability of idea cognition which arises from the pre-existence of the soul, it also concerns the language and notions proper to it. It is connected with the conviction that intellect, while being a part of reality is a product of this reality and therefore, it is capable of describing that reality. The description is accomplished by means of notions. Everything which constitutes the truth about reality itself, is and may be solely the recollection of its structure, expressed by language. Therefore, one can speak about a particular relationship between the structure of language and the structure of reality. The conviction appears that examining the structure of reality may be accomplished through examining the proper relationships occurring between the notions of language which describes and expresses this structure. Plato realised the prominence of such analyses. He related them to the content of the fundamental method of philosophical activity, the dialectal method. Basically it concerned two problems. The first one is connected with "reading" the nature of the world, and thus with the question: what modes of being are present in them? The second one referred to the necessity of analysis of the world structure which is always accomplished by the power of intellect and notions related to it. Plato proposes a precise

---

[4] See Plato; *Meno* 81c, 86b; *Phaedo* 73b–74a; *Phaedrus* 249bd. On the anamnetic process see B. Dembiński, *Teoria idei. Ewolucja myśli Platońskiej*, Katowice 1997, p. 99.

method of examining relationships between notions which will allow to establish which notions may interconnect, which connect necessarily and which are totally impossible. In "Sophist" dialogue he presents an example of such analysis.[5] It is the analysis of relationships which occur between the highest generic notions (μέγιστα γένη). Plato mentions the following genera: being, identity, difference, movement and rest. In his opinion every analysed state of things, irrespective of the fact whether it exists as real, ideal or mental, is characterized by the fact that in a certain way it *is* (exists). Thus, we grasp it as ideal, real or mental being. Each being is something which it is and it is different form another being. Each time then, identity and difference are inherent in it. Similarly, since every being is either in *motion* or at rest (ideal or mental being is not in its existence dependent on the dynamics of spatiotemporal structures) and movement or rest is inherent in it. Surely, more such generic notions may be mentioned. In "Sophist" for the needs of defining a sophist, Plato uses the indicated five generic notions. The starting point is the conviction that sophistry is the way of creating delusive images. Therefore, immediately appears the problem of relationships between what is and what merely seems to be that thing. It directly leads to the issues of truth and falsity, true and false sentences and judgements.[6] That is why the highest necessity turns out to be the examination of relationships between generic notions exemplified by Plato.

I propose the analysis of notions of being and non-being, identity and difference, rest and movement. It allows to ultimately define a sophist as a person who is able to create false images. However, with the appearance of falsity, there appears the question about possibility of its existence, since in such a case, says Plato, one must assume that there exists something which does not exist. Then the existence of non-being must be recognized. The thesis of Parmenides of Elea which expresses the fundamental conviction of Greeks that non-being does not exist, would have to be questioned. Therefore, it must be considered what is being and what is non-being which appears in deliberations. They are generic notions. Plato becomes convicted through an analysis that with the notion of non-being one may connect merely

[5] Plato, *Sophist*, 240d–262e.
[6] *Ibidem*, 236d, 237a.

something which constitutes so-called relative non-being, i.e. non-being which may be understood only as the opposite of being, whereas it cannot be understood as its contradiction. Nobody is able to comprehend non-being as the contradiction of being. Since even contemplating non-being makes non-being exist, as contemplated. Thus, such non-being consistently cannot be even contemplated. Something which is, exists, and cannot not exist. Non-being is a function of thinking and not the state of reality. This in turn which exists, each time is something which it is (identity) and concurrently it is not something different, through which it is distinguished from that which is different (difference). Therefore, difference and identity must inhere in every being. Thus, in every being it should be determined what is the source of its identity and what is the basis of its distinction in relation to other beings. It should be also considered if the being which we mean is a real being (spatiotemporal) or an ideal one. For on that basis we can attribute to it movement or rest. All the relationships mentioned by Plato are the necessary condition to conduct analyses. Every kind of conceptual connections should be considered, as they may, if examined properly, lead to grasping the essence of things which constitutes the aim and subject of our study. Plato refers to the example of language and music, showing that knowledge of their structure emerges from the analysis of relationships which occur between their basic elements, which are letters and sounds,[7] notions and sentences, intervals, rhythms and cadences. To know the structure of language or music is to know how the forming elements are related in it, to know which of them combine with one another, which may combine and which combinations are totally impossible. A similar way of thinking is typical to other languages, too. The language of mathematics can be an example.

It is apparent, however, that in essence it is proper to every form of science. Therefore, Plato treats the dialectical method as a universal method. It is obvious that within the sphere of particular sciences we will always deal with generic notions characteristic of these sciences and whose analysis we should conduct precisely. Plato presents such conviction in

---

[7] *Ibidem*, 252e–253b.

"Theaetetus"[8] dialogue. He claims that knowledge is an effect of process of analysis in which the decisive role is played by analysis of relationships occurring between notions which express simple elements of experience, denominated by Plato as elements (στοιχεῖα). Those elements are the result of sensuous cognition which presents the knower with merely beliefs (δόξα) and convictions about their veracity (ἀληθὴς δόξα). Knowledge appears only as a result of the rational depiction of proper relations between elements. Above all it is about the ways of concatenation of notions by means of logical reasoning.

Plato calls those relationships "nexuses" (συμπλοκή) and they concern notions.[9] The strict depiction is thus the examination of modes of their relationships. By examining the relationships at the level of notions we try to reconstruct the structures which are proper to the states of things examined by Intellect. Plato again makes use of examples from the domains of language and music and he says that the examination of elements, letters or sounds alone does not constitute knowledge yet. This appears only when we are able to grasp the proper and relevant relationships between the elements. Therefore, only familiarity with grammar and theory of music gives us knowledge because only they explain precisely the modes of concatenation of elements. However, in "Theaetetus" an idea appears to solve another problem which will soon arise in philosophical deliberations. Plato remarks that apart from the familiarity of concatenations and relations between elements we should also have the knowledge of something which is common to definite states of things and something which distinguishes these states and thereby constitutes their individuality. Knowledge ought to be thus the knowledge of something which is common and the knowledge of something which is unitary. In the first case, we consider the predicate comprising many subjects and common qualities of those subjects. In the second case, there appears the necessity of allowing for something which determines a certain state of things in its individuality and which Plato will name in "Theaetetus" the unitary difference (διαφορότητα ἄρα).[10] Thereby,

[8] Plato, *Theaetetus*, 196a–210d.

[9] *Ibidem*, 202b

[10] Plato, *Theaetetus*, 209d.

it appears the division into generic and specific notions. Genera comprehend common qualities, species indicate unitary qualities. Species are subordinate to genera. The study will concern then the analysis of relationships which occur between genera and species.[11] Aristotle followed these intuitions and decided to consider them while proposing his own solutions. He became thereby a continuator of Platonic tradition.

He admitted that species emerge from genera and differences (ἐκ τοῦ γένους καὶ διαφόρων τὰ εἴδη). He claimed that the generic predicate is incomplete, does not exhaust the definite content of subject (merely indicates its potential component). It is made only by the specific predicate which directs cognition to the essence of the subject. In Aristotle's view, the exact definition of the substance (in cognition of reality it is always the second substance) demands specification and this, in turn, may be accomplished by means of specific and generic predicates as well as specific differences. For example, man is defined as a rational animal where man is the indication of species, animal – genus, and rational is the indication of the specific difference.

Afterwards Porfirius and John Duns Scotus went even further. The first one adopted the highest and lowest genus (dividing dichotomically the category of substance into adequately assigned generalities, which are genera and species and which together with the specific difference make up predicates – *quincque voces*) building the hierarchical system of notions called Porfirius' tree. Whereas Scotus arranged reality in the hierarchical ontic system placing on its top the highest, non-contradictive nature of being which ultimately, passing through more and more perfect essences-natures, concentrates on the actual, inimitable individuality (*haeccecitas*).

---

[11] "The one who can do it, that duly perceives how one form extends through many genera, although each of them lies separately. And how many genera different from one another one form comprises, and how one form through many genera joins in one, and how many it distinguishes, determined from every side. This is what knowledge consists in, it allows to resolve on each genus, if and how it may connect with others, or if and how not. [...] to divide things into genera and neither to take the same genus for another nor another one for the same, won't we say that it is the matter of dialectical knowledge?" (trans. by W. Witwicki), Plato, *Sophist*, 253de.

After presenting the aforementioned issues we may return once again to categories and consider their place in the system of Aristotle's philosophy. First of all, it ought to be noticed that Aristotle concatenated the notion of category with the basic modes of existence of the substance. He also joined them with forms of predication. He analysed categories as grammatical forms of the natural language. The notion of category (used in the Aristotle's work "Categories") constitutes the direct reference to Plato's thought and his conception of the highest genera. Genera were to express predicates common to many subjects. Plato distinguished only some, naming them the highest genera. In Aristotle's case, Platonic conception of genera was transformed into the conception of necessary properties and modes of being inherent in every actually existing substance. They will be denominated as categories by Aristotle. He distinguished the following categories: the substance itself as a subject of cosmic qualities and modes of being inherent in it, quantity, quality, ratio, place, time, location, disposition, activity and passive affections. The reason for Aristotle's distinction of ten categories is unknown. It could be merely presumed that they constitute the articulations of modes wherein an actual, truly existent substance exists in the world and they are an attempt to describe them precisely, which allows to distinguish one substance from the other. A vital role was assuredly played by linguistic considerations as well, when in the process of articulating of the examined states of things it was necessary to refer to notions which describe these states.[12]

A more complete comprehension of the role performed in Aristotle's reflection by categories may be accomplished from the perspective of notions which refer to dispensable qualities of the substance which Aristotle denominates as indispositions (συμβεβηκότα). For example, the category of quality must inhere in a given substance, provided it is a truly existent substance, however it does not necessarily have to be the strictly determined quality, e.g. a definite colour. It may be various colours. Thus, there appears the division into necessary and unnecessary modes of existence

[12] I avail myself of an interesting discussion on categories in *Powszechna encyklopedia filozofii*, prepared by A. Maryniarczyk, Lublin 2004, T. V, pp. 539–545.

of the substance. Aristotle names the first as categories and the second indispositions. The first ones are invariable and necessary, the second variable and unnecessary. It seems that thereby Aristotle tried to join diverse threads of philosophical tradition when it was contended whether reality is in its essence variable or invariable, necessary or unnecessary. Aristotle admitted that substance may possess both features. It accounts for the basis of predication on three genera of substances. The first ones are sensible substances which arise and perish, the second ones are sensible substances but imperishable (sky, planets, stars), the third ones are immobile substances, eternal (God, substances moving respective celestial spheres).

Apart from ontological issues, a significant role in comprehension of the notion of Aristotelian category is played by the linguistic context wherein substance is predicated. We ought to dispense in it with notions which correspond to determinate modes of being of substance in order that this being could be precisely articulated. Whereas that is directly connected with the language wherein this cognition is manifested. Categories become the fundamental structures of language whereby the depiction of substance is accomplished. Therefore their analysis is necessary. It refers to both the modes of creating notions, functions of notions, as well as the modes of their concatenation. It is also about the comprehension and capability of applying them. In "Posterior Analytics" and "Topics" Aristotle analyses the modes wherein general notions refer to the objects which they predicate. The fundamental notions are here species, genus, attribute, difference and indisposition. These notions make up the rudimentary components of language whereon grammar is based. It has a vital effect on the syntactic structure of language. It also affects semantics and pragmatics of language.

A separate issue concerns the ontological context of comprehension of category. It is about the aforementioned modes of being of substance. Aristotle endeavours to propose an original comprehension of being whereon he says that it may be expressed in many different ways (τὸ δὲ ὂν λέγεται μὲν πολλαχῶς).[13] It is the consequence of an attempt to concatenate many previous threads of Greek philosophical tradition wherein the notion of being was grasped in many different ways. Some believed that

[13] Aristotle, *Metaphysics*, 1003a30.

being is constant and invariable, others claimed that it is solely variable, yet others proposed mixed states. Aristotle acknowledged that in their own ways all of them were right. For being can be predicated multifariously because various modes of being and various qualities (necessary and unnecessary) inhere in them. Therefore, being may be both substance in the context of particular categories, as well as being may be substance in the context of a definite indisposition, but being may be also substance as form and matter. Being may be also substance in reference to ability and act inherent in it. The point is, that while analysing substance and categories inherent in it, to make the precise establishment as to which particular forms of it are typical of a given substance. Using a present-day example, let us consider two electrons. They are indistinguishable with regard to structure. But they are not the same, then speaking of two electrons would not be possible, though. The similar categories, characteristic of all spatiotemporal being inhere in them. But with regard to, for example, categories of time and space they are different. As far as the category of time and space is inherent in one and the other, each of them individually has another substantiation of it, another indisposition. This allows to distinguish precisely one electron from another. Categories and indispositions become then the condition of discrimination between one substance and the other and the condition of defining identity of each of them. That is what philosophical examination consists in. It has to be established what is common and distinguish what is discriminatory. Categories and indispositions fulfil this task in a precise way. The metaphysical analysis of substance turns out to be necessary in that case. Its next stages become related to the establishment of form organising the indeterminate primary matter, which when subjected to organisation becomes transformed into the secondary matter. The matter itself is comprehended as the ability wherein all forms are potentially present. The outcome is a concrete substance which is a compound (σύνολον) of form and matter. Its origin is enabled by either internal causes (matter and form) or external causes (causal and intentional). The metaphysical analysis which is a non-contradictory analysis (ratiocinations conducted therein are based on the principle of contradiction which cannot be infringed) reflects on substance in all its constituent elements and concatenations which occur among those elements. It allows to analyse precisely the structure and being of each particular substance and determine the actual and ultimate aim of philosophical studies.

It is also apparent that the conception of category constitutes a natural continuation of Platonic conception of the highest genera,[14] which in the later history of philosophy will become converted into the theory of predicates defining the ontic content of predicated subjects (Porfirius' tree) and a hierarchical attempt to arrange the forms of nature accomplished by John Duns Scotus, from the most extensive forms (being – non-contradiction) to individual ones (*haecceitas*). Concurrently, the scholastics minutely distinguished six basic categories which they denominated as predicaments. They are the following categories: being-essence, quality, quantity, movement-change, ratio and possession. In modern times philosophers adopted various genera of categories: R. Descartes and J. Locke adopted three: substance, location and relations, J.S. Mill four: feelings, souls, bodies and ratios, W. Wundt four: things, qualities, states and ratios.[15] The most prominent comprehension of categories was connected, above all, with philosophy of I. Kant for whom they were the primary and chief forms of thinking which allow to unite diverse representations. Today, the notion of category is most often associated with the theoretical-multitudinous conception comprising the hierarchy of category of sets of various type. Thereby, the notion of category retained its topicality until today. Thus again the conviction is confirmed, that the intuitions proposed by ancient philosophers account for the basis of comprehension and the mode of predication of the world examined by us. One should perceive therein their indispensability and necessity of constant reference to origins wherefrom they derive their imperishable obligatoriness.

---

[14] It may be acknowledged that such a situation tends to be the reason for misunderstandings which appear in an interpretation of the Platonic doctrine. For the objection of treating ideas as a hypostasized notion seems to result from the lack of distinction of the notion of idea from the idea itself. Idea is not a notion but it is expressed in a notion. This notion is certainly a general one, a mode of articulating ideas. However, it cannot mean that the idea itself is a notion or a hypostasized notion. For no notion can be the cause of existence and ontic determinacy of any actual state of things.

[15] I make use of findings of A. Podsiad, *Słownik terminów i pojęć filozoficznych*, Warszawa 2000, p. 435.

Dariusz Olesiński

Plato's Conception of the Good in *The Republic*

ABSTRACT: In Book II of *The Republic,* Plato distinguishes three forms of the good:
- good only in itself,
- good both in itself and for its consequences,
- good only for its consequences (*Rep.* 357b–d).

Choosing the second form, he emphasizes a twofold nature of the Good, i.e. absolute and relative one, which turns out to be crucial for a proper understanding of his subsequent characteristics in Books VI and VII, especially expressed with the use of the analogy of the sun. Presented from this perspective, the supremacy of the Good over other ideas (its being ἐπέκεινα τῆς οὐσίας), does not mean absolute existential transcendence but it indicates its ultimate status, which results really from a twofold nature of the Good, and which is predominantly expressed by the impact power (δύναμις) inherent to the Good. Hence, the presentation of the Good in categories of the cause (αἰτία), which function in three fundamental orders of reality (the metaphysical, epistemological, and practical one), turns out to be the most important for Plato's conception.

The conception of the good which is introduced in *The Republic* can be understood mainly in the epistemological context as the culmination of Plato's quest for the foundation of ἐπιστήμη, which was initiated *expressis verbis* in *Meno,* or to be more precise, in a passage where Socrates says:

> [...] for true opinions (δόξαι ἀληθεῖς), as long as they remain, are a fine thing and all they do is good, but they are not willing to remain long, and they escape from a man's mind, so that they are not worth much until one ties them down by giving an account of the reason why (αἰτίας λογισμῷ). And that, Meno my friend, is recollection (ἀνάμνησις), as we previously agreed. After they are tied down, in the first place they become knowledge, and then they remain in place. That is why knowledge is prized higher than correct opinion (τιμιώτερον ἐπιστήμη ὀρθῆς δόξης ἐστίν), differs from correct opinion in being tied down (δεσμῷ).[1]

Tying down opinions with the reason why (αἰτίας λογισμῷ), suggests that it is necessary to find a proper cause of knowledge. However, the role of an anamnetic process indicated in the text is to facilitate a direct passage from true opinions to knowledge, but the process requires explaining its foundation by referring to the question of a real and final cause which enables to tie down opinions, which would transfer them into valuable knowledge.

In *Phaedo*, this ties (δεσμός) are allusively identified with the Good, or more precisely, the power of its impact. When Socrates observes that the vast majority of people is not able to find the proper cause (αἰτία) of things, he emphasizes that

> [...] as for their capacity (δύναμιν) of being in the best place they could possibly be put, this they do not look for, nor do they believe it to have any divine force, [...] and they do not believe that the truly good and 'binding' binds and holds them

[1] Plato, *Meno,* 97e–98a. All quotes from Plato's dialogues cited from: *Plato: Complete Works: Edited with Introduction and Notes*, eds. J.M. Cooper, D.S. Hutchinson, Indianapolis and Cambridge 1997.

together (ὡς ἀληθῶς τὸ ἀγαθὸν καὶ δέον συνδεῖν καὶ συνέχειν οὐδὲν οἴονται).[2]

The initial characteristics of the good as something that possesses the power of true binding, then becomes a basis for further considerations on its nature, which occur in *The Republic.* Finally, they lead (in Books VI and VII) to indicating a fundamental role of the idea of the Good as a primary principle (ἀρχή) functioning in three basic orders of reality (the metaphysical, epistemological and practical one), and the cause (αἰτία) of everything that is just and beautiful (ὀρθῶν τε καὶ καλῶν).[3]

However, before it takes place, as a part of considerations on the essence of justice in Book II, Plato performs the important classification of three forms (εἴδη) of what can be defined as goods, and he enumerates them as follows:

- good only in itself (αὐτὸ αὑτοῦ ἕνεκα);
- good both in itself and for its consequences (αὐτό τε αὑτοῦ … καὶ τῶν ἀπ' αὐτοῦ γιγνομένων);
- good only for its consequences (γίγνεται ἀπ' αὐτῶν).[4]

Contrary to his interlocutor Glaucon, who quotes the opinion of the majority (πολλοῖς) and chooses justice only due to benefits which it brings, Socrates is in favor of the second of enumerated forms of the good evaluating it as the most beautiful (κάλλίστος).[5] The form chosen by him, i.e. the good in itself and for its consequences, suggests that the nature of the good is complex, and it must involve ability to affect (δύναμις) the external reality.

Thus, the twofold nature of the Good is singled out (the absolute and relative one), which can be accepted as a paradigm determining the scope of its correct understanding as well as its further, more detailed characteristic presented in Books VI and VII. In this central part of the dialogue, Plato shows causative functions of the idea of the Good mainly using the image of the sun, where the sun is presented metaphorically as a son of the

---

[2] Plato, *Phaedo,* 99c.

[3] See *Rep.* 511, 517c.

[4] See *Rep.* 357b–d.

[5] See *Rep.* 358a.

Good.[6] In this way, the relations between a father and a son is employed to express the analogy of a position and function formed by two ontologically and axiologically different contents of the following classes: superior, represented by the father (the noetic order), and inferior, represented by the son (the phenomenal order).

Generally, the structure of a metaphor is as follows: the sun as the light source is also the condition for seeing, or the cognitive relation which occurs between the eye and sensual objects.[7] Moreover, it does not only give light (hence, being *causa cognoscienti* of the sensual world), but also heat, thus it contributes to feeding and development, therefore to the birth (γένεσις) of sensual things, and fulfills the role of *causa efficiens.*[8] The first part of the metaphor transferred *per analogiam* to a noetic dimension illustrates a cognitive relation, whereas the second one a metaphysical relation. The Good binds the objects of knowledge (ideas), truth and being,[9] on the one hand, as the cause of knowledge and truth which enables the cognition of being.[10] On the other hand, it binds them as the cause of being and the essence of an idea[11] in the metaphysical order.

However, certain interpretational problems are linked to Plato's analogy based on solar metaphors, which focuses on the question of a distinctive status of the nature of the Good, and its relation to the ideal and phenomenal world. Such a problem is posed, for example, by a proper understanding of generating ideas, which corresponds to the process of γένεσις present in the empirical order (κόσμος αἰσθητός). The Good provides ideas with being and essence,[12] however as eternal and unchanging beings by definition, and therefore uncreated, contrary to phenomenal things, they cannot be characterized by coming into being and perishing. This indicates a certain inconsistency within the solar analogy, namely, if the function fulfilled by the sun for phenomena can be explained using the concept of an efficient

---

6 *Rep*. 506e–509b.

7 *Rep*. 508b–509a.

8 *Rep*. 509b.

9 *Rep*. 508d.

10 *Rep*. 508e.

11 *Rep*. 509b.

12 *Rep*. 509b.

cause (*causa efficiens*), it cannot certainly apply to the relation of the Good toward ideas. Therefore, in what sense could the Good contribute to the genesis of eternal and unchanging objects within κόσμος νοητός?

In the opinion of Mario Vegetti, this problem is only apparently paradoxical since the Good properly ensures the ideal existence of ideas, it ensures also the essence and truth, the consistency and ontological stability which turns them into true, normative and paradigmatic objects.[13] That is why "generating" ideas does not involve the transition from non-existence toward existence but it involves cognitive manifestation of truth determined by a polar tension between a subject and an object (subjectivity and objectivity, in other words), it is primarily epistemological not metaphysical.

However, it should be mentioned that ideas become epistemologically attractive objects, i.e. proper objects of knowledge able to found ἐπιστήμη, just due to their existential status, namely, because they are unchanging and true objects in the ontological order, and these attributes result from their participation in the idea of the Good. This leads to a basic controversial issue which is related to the question of a distinguished status of the Good, especially in an ontological sense.

An attempt to answer the above question requires introductory reference to make a distinction between the ideal and specific attributes of ideas.[14] Since the idea of the Good is the only idea which introduces the

---

[13] See M. Vegetti, *Megiston Mathema. L'idea del 'buono' e le sue funzione,* [in:] *Platone,* La Repubblica, vol. V, ed. M. Vegetti, Libro VI–VII, Napoli 2003, p. 272.

[14] This distinction, though differently conceptualized, has been introduced, among others, by G. Vlastos, D. Keyt, G. Santas, M. Dixsaut, Ch. Shields. See G. Vlastos, *Degrees of Reality in Plato,* [in:] G. Vlastos, *Platonic Studies*, Princeton 1973, pp. 58–75; D. Keyt, *Plato's Paradox that the Immutable Is Unknowable,* "Philosophical Quarterly" 1969, 19 (74), pp. 1–14; G. Santas, *The Form of the Good in Plato's Republic*, [in:] *Plato 1: Metaphysics and Epistemology*, ed. G. Fine, New York 1999, pp. 247–274; M. Dixsaut, *Encore une fois le bien,* [in:] *Études sur la republique de Platon. vol. 2 de la science, du bien et des mythes*, Paris 2005, pp. 225–255; Ch. Shields, *Surpassing in Dignity and Power: The Metaphysics of Goodness in Plato's Republic*, [in:] *Socratic, Platonic and Aristotelian Studies: Essays in Honor of Gerasimos Santas,* ed. G. Anagnostopoulos, Dodrecht – Heidelberg – London – New York 2011, pp. 281–296. Moreover, Vlatos and Keyt have observed that this distinction can be also found in Aristotle's *Topics* (137b67).

causative relations not only for phenomena but also for other ideas (participating in it as a meta-ideas), this means that it gives them nonspecific attributes which belong to all ideas. Hence, the conception according to which we should distinguish between the attributes of the ideas as ideas rooted in the Good, or rather as ideal attributes, and their own proper attributes, i.e. attributes possessed by every idea, and which are guaranteed by being this very, proper idea (resp. the idea of something) seems justified.

For better understanding of this distinction between ideal and proper attributes (and in consequence, the functions which are fulfilled by the Good towards ideas), the example of the idea of a wheel will be used.[15] Ideal attributes of such an idea, like any other idea, concern its being an idea, understood as an intelligible, unchanging, essential, necessary, absolute, non-gradable being.[16] While, proper attributes of the idea of a wheel amount to a proper content which constitutes wheelness as wheelness in its maximum, essential purity.

To be a wheel, a sensual object must participate in the idea of the wheel, and this participation is nothing other than only possessing some proper attributes (*proprium*) of the idea of the wheel which constitute "being round." Hence, the idea of the Good interferes here with phenomena only in an indirect manner, namely, constituting ideal attributes of all ideas, which decide about their being an intelligible object. However, to be a *good* (*resp.* perfect) wheel, a sensual object must, to a certain extent, also participate in the ideal attributes of the idea of a wheel, which in turn result from the participation of the idea of a wheel in the idea of the Good. The fact that a phenomenon participates in ideal attributes makes it better to such extent, to which this participation takes place, since ideal attributes are the factors which have decided in the idea of its being a supreme being

---

[15] See G. Santas, *op. cit.*, p. 264.

[16] These attributes occur repeatedly in *Corpus Platonicum* when the status of ideas is characterized. A key passage from *Symposium* can be a good example of their abundance – See *Symp.* 210e–211b. For Plato, a fundamental synonym of perfection is unchangeability, which is expressed in many parts of his dialogue, See, e.g. *Rep.* 381b: "Whatever is in good condition (καλῶς ἔχον), then, whether by nature or craft or both, admits least of being changed by anything else". See also *Rep.* 380e.

of a definite content. In other words, to be *good*, a sensual wheel must not only participate in the idea of the Good, but also in *goodness* of the idea of a wheel, and only this makes it a *perfect* wheel to some extent.

Due to possessing ideal attributes, ideas express the Good, indicating perfection, here being the best of all possible wheels. Since it is possible to graduate the intensity of participation of the sensual in the intelligible, let us notice that participation only in proper attributes of the idea of a wheel cannot turn a sensual object into a *good* (possibly *the best*) wheel because proper attributes of the idea of a wheel do not refer to the idea of the Good, since they do not participate in it. In light of above findings, we can also observe that the distinction between opinions and knowledge,[17] which is discussed in Book V of *The Republic*, the distinction which is both referring to and developing an earlier mentioned motif from *Meno* concerning the quest for an epistemic fundament of true opinions (δόξαι ἀληθεῖς), is based on the criterion of ideal attributes of cognitive objects. Due to the lack of these attributes, sensual things cannot be objects of knowledge (ἐπιστήμη), but only opinions (δόξα).[18]

Upon understanding the nature of the Good from which ideas derive their essence and being, it can be concluded that their ideal attributes are simultaneously proper attributes of the idea of the Good, from which their ideality, or being an idea, and consequently their essence (οὐσία) are derived. Thus the idea of the Good can be understood as a formal cause (*causa formalis*) of ideas,[19] being the cause of their existence and essence, as well as their cognizability. The bonds (δεσμός) which are sought after in *Meno,* needed for consolidation of true opinions, and for their transformation into knowledge due to causative relation, can be identified with ideal attributes of ideas, being at the same time an objective criterion of knowledge. Since the Good is responsible for these ideal attributes, as their cause, thus it is what finally founds ἐπιστήμη.

---

[17] See *Rep.* 476c–480a.

[18] As it is observed by Socrates: "No matter how many ways we examine it, what is completely (παντελῶς) is completely knowable (παντελῶς γνωστόν) and what is in no way is in every way unknowable (ἄγνωστον)", *Rep.* 477a.

[19] See G. Santas, *op. cit.*, p. 255.

Comments on ideal attributes of ideas and participation of sensual objects in them allow us to indicate one more important relationship, justifying Plato's belief in the twofold nature of the Good. Namely, in Book I of *The Republic* Plato introduced a different criterion of the Good than the one outlined in the central Books, according to which value of a thing (and consequently, its being good) is not estimated by its participation in ideal attributes of ideas, but by the extent of a degree of the compliance with its inherent function, and the function the thing is to fulfill.[20] Thus, it is both a functional and instrumental concept of the good which seems to deny its ideal and essential presentation. However, as it is argued by Gerasimos Santas, for Plato "function always follows form",[21] these two presentations of the Good can be naturally combined. Let us observe that the more sensual objects resemble ideal attributes of their ideas (they are becoming the good in the sense of αὐτὸ αὐτοῦ), the more they fulfill their inherent function (they are becoming the good in the sense of ἀπ' αὐτοῦ γιγνομένων).

Therefore, we go back to the formerly presented distinction of three forms of the good in Book II, and to distinguishing its twofold nature. Now, we can understand why this form of the good was chosen by Plato as a proper presentation of its nature, connecting an essential aspect with the functional-instrumental one. The first, autotelic concept does not recognize a dynamic aspect of the Good as real power (δύναμις) able to form the world, especially in its practical and ethical dimension. In turn, the last, purely instrumental concept lacks appropriate measure which can determine what is really useful. In this way, Plato stresses that in order to understand the nature of the Good adequately these two presentations (the autotelic and instrumental one, the absolute and relative one, the theoretic and pragmatic one) must not only be accounted for, but also they must be agreed on harmoniously, and this harmony can be achieved thanks to the fact that the Good is cognized by the category of cause (αἰτία).

A pragmatic aspect reveals that the Good, as the cause of everything that is just and beautiful, does not limit its power to the area of κόσμος

[20] See *Rep*. 352e–353a.

[21] G. Santas, *op. cit*., p. 266.

νοητός but sets an aim for sensual things to the extent to which they participate in the ideas which are the model of perfection for them. It is possible to evaluate sensual things only by recognizing (ἀνάμνησις) the idea which explains their *raison d'être*, or in other words their sense, understood functionally as useful application. Thus, as it is stressed by Plato, somebody who wants to act wisely (ἐμφρόνως πράξειν) in private and public life must have an insight (ἰδεῖν) into the intelligible world, which offers truth and reason (ἀλήθειαν καὶ νοῦν).[22]

Therefore, truth and knowledge themselves do not possess the aim, since theoretical knowledge must act in accordance with the Good, which is only possible when the idea of the Good is not merely a coordinating idea which gives meaning to all other ideas within κόσμος νοητός, but also it is able to regulate human life by making people act properly within κόσμος αἰσθητός. However, it leads to another interpretational difficulty because the Good can fulfill this role only when it is cognitively accessible to man.

Meanwhile, Plato emphasizes that the idea of the Good is not directly and completely cognizable, and its knowledge is burdened with toil:

> But this is how I see it: In the knowable realm, the form of the good is the last thing to be seen, and it is reached only with difficulty (μόγις ὁρᾶσθαι). Once one has seen it, however, one must conclude that it is the cause (αἰτία) of all (πάντων) that is correct and beautiful (ὀρθῶν τε καὶ καλῶν) in anything, that it produces both light and its source in the visible realm, and that in the intelligible realm it controls and provides truth and understanding, so that anyone who is to act sensibly in private or public must see it.[23]

Although the idea of the Good belongs to the realm of the cognizable (ἐν τῷ γνωστῷ),[24] it belongs to its extreme (τελευταία), it is located as τέλος of the noetic activity (τῷ τοῦ νοητοῦ τέλει),[25] being as if a border point from which synoptic knowledge, which is accessible only to an assidu-

[22] See *Rep.* 517c.
[23] *Rep.* 517b–c.
[24] *Rep.* 517b.
[25] See *Rep.* 532b.

ous dialectician, spreads out. As the result, it sets a task for a process of knowledge, and the realization of its ultimate aim.[26]

Taking into account the perfection of the Good itself, its completeness, and also imperfection of any other good, it becomes clear why Plato claims that the proper way of philosophical development requires constant maintaining this Good as the ultimate and highest aim of knowledge, and that without knowing it, it is impossible to know any other good. Every man aims at what is the best, but the degree of participation in goodness of this perfect Good is the only certain measure of goodness for all things. As it is stressed by Socrates:

> [...] any measure of such things that falls short in any way of that which is is not good measure, for nothing incomplete is the measure of anything (ἀτελὲς γὰρ οὐδὲν οὐδενὸς μέτρον), although people are sometimes of the opinion that an incomplete treatment is nonetheless adequate and makes further investigation unnecessary.[27]

That is why the relation between a theoretical order and a practical one (between "to know the good" and "to do the good"), which is emphasized by Plato and which can realize itself only thanks to the idea of the Good, becomes understandable only when we remember that knowing the Good was not conceived by him as a final result of a single process of argumentation, the result which is related to certainty guaranteed by correctness of deductive reasoning. Plato meant rather a continuous, repeated, existential process of gaining an understanding by its gradual deepening within the dialectical process of knowledge of the hermeneutical nature.[28] Hence, all understanding is gradable, i.e. in relation to an object it is more or less inquisitive, and in relation to a subject it is more or less conscious. Knowledge of the Good is ultimately possible provided that we

---

[26] See M. Vegetti, *op. cit.*, p. 275.

[27] *Rep.* 504c.

[28] See D. Olesiński, *Symfonia logosu w Platońskim „Fedonie"*, [in:] *Postacie i funkcje logosu w filozofii greckiej*, eds. D. Kubok, D. Olesiński, Katowice – Bielsko-Biała 2011, pp. 59–72.

will conceive it as understanding, and consequently, not using categories of certainty but those of a process of improving the insight[29].

Thereby, the Good appears as a foundation of ἐπιστήμη in a twofold sense, i.e. not only as its ultimate aim (the end of cognitive activity), but also as an always assumed principle facilitating knowledge. Let us observe that a real cognition of any object depends on our ability to ideate it, namely, to distinguish it in itself from its imperfect manifestations which occur both as sensual perception and in our imagination. However, this ideation is inextricably connected to the knowledge of the Good, since it is the cause of ideal attributes of ideas.

A dialectician must be then able to separate the Good from all that only presupposes this Good as a principle of its existence and intelligibility, he must be able to separate its absolute from a relative aspect:

> [...] unless someone can distinguish in an account (διορίσασθαι τῷ λόγῳ) the form of the good (ἀγαθοῦ ἰδέαν) from everything else, can survive all refutation, as if in a battle, striving to judge things not in accordance with opinion but in accordance with being (κατ' οὐσίαν), and can come through all this with his account still intact, you'll say that he doesn't know the good itself (αὐτὸ τὸ ἀγαθόν) or any other good (ἄλλο ἀγαθόν)[30].

At the same time, the Good cannot be an object of knowledge in the sense a being, or an idea is because it is itself a principle which facilitates all cognition of ideas. Thereby, it is not directly recognized as an object external to a wheel, but rather as a real cause which facilitates its cognition, or as an ultimate reason of this cognition. In other words, the ideation, which is a central moment of such an activity, as presupposing the presence of the Good, is what, in an indirect manner, reveals best the Good in the cognitive order.

---

[29] As it is expressed by J. Cooper: "Knowledge here, as usual in Plato, is taken to entail understanding, so that to know, e.g., a good life is not just to know which life is good, and from what points of view or in what circumstances, and so on, but precisely to understand what this goodness itself is that one attributes to it with these qualifications", J. Cooper, *The Psychology of Justice in Plato*, "American Philosophical Quarterly", April 1977, 14:2, p. 154.

[30] *Rep*. 534b–c.

A distinguished status of the idea of the Good is also reflected in the choice of expressions indicating its axiological primarity, since Plato calls it the "brightest" (φανότατον), "happiest" (εὐδαιμονέστατον) and "best among the things that are" (ἀρίστου ἐν τοῖς οὖσι).[31] However, the phrase from the passage, according to which the Good is not a being (οὐσία), but something beyond being (ἐπέκεινα τῆς οὐσίας) is the most frequently commented on and the most interpretively controversial:

> [...] therefore, you should also say that not only do the objects of knowledge owe their being known to the good, but their being is also due to it, although the good is not being (οὐκ οὐσίας ὄντος τοῦ ἀγαθοῦ), but superior to it in rank and power (ἐπέκεινα τῆς οὐσίας πρεσβείᾳ καὶ δυνάμει ὑπερέχοντος).[32]

The above quoted passage seems to be contradictory to many other passages of the dialogue in which the Good is defined as an idea (ἀγαθόν ἰδέα), and which indicate its nature as a real dialectical aim of knowledge,[33] whereas, in light of the passage, we could advocate for a transcendental, nonbeing status of the Good. Beside Neoplatonic tradition, we can include into this interpretative trend a modern stand of the Tübingen School, represented by supporters of the esoteric character of Plato's philosophy. It is characteristic for this interpretation to identify, according to the theory of ἄγραφα δόγματα,[34] the One from the theory of principles with the Good

---

[31] See *Rep.* 518c, 526e, 532c, respectively.

[32] *Rep.* 509b.

[33] See especially *Rep.* 505a, 532b.

[34] Acceptation of the thesis which identifies the Good with the One results in not basing a reading of Plato on his own dialogues but on Aristotle's and other indirect testimonies. Such an objection against an esoteric interpretation is made by Lafrance; See Y. Lafrance, *Deux lectures de l'Idée du Bien chez Platon:* République *502c–509*, "Laval théologique et philosophique" 2006, vol. 62, No 2, pp. 262–263. Isnardi Parente is of similar opinion, indicating the hypothesis of Plato's non-written science is historically weakly rooted, and arguing that the testimonies of indirect tradition do not allow to reconstruct Plato's thought coherently; See M. Isnardi Parente, *Testimonia Platonica*, vol. 1, *Le testimonianze di Aristotele*, Roma 1997, pp. 403–405.

from *The Republic,* to emphasize its radical transcendence in relation to being at the same time.[35]

Let us observe that according to the earlier mentioned Platonic solar analogy, the sun is not "beyond" the realm of κόσμος αἰσθητός being something invisible, but it remains a sensual, observable object. Thus the Good should be conceived analogically, to the extent to which it is an intelligible object, it cannot completely transcend the sphere of κόσμος νοητός, since then it would become totally inaccessible for an intellectual cognition and undermine Plato's intention to make from the Good an object of the highest knowledge (μέγιστον μάθημα),[36] as well as the foundation of ἐπιστήμη. Since the sun is a sensual being, just the brightest one, as a source of light which enables to see, it can itself be seen with difficulty. A corresponding situation is observed in case of the idea of the Good, which in relation to other ideas, turns out to be more transparent, and that is why it appears as something difficult to grasp (μόγις ὁρᾶσθαι),[37] something whose achievement requires from a neophyte choosing a long and tedious way, which is to lead to possible development of a dialectic ability to the full.[38]

Moreover, if we analyze this full passage, thus if we do not take a huge fragment away from its context, we can observe that the Good is not ἐπέκεινα τῆς οὐσίας in an absolute way (in every possible respect),

---

[35] See especially: H.J. Krämer, *Epekeina tes ousias. Zu Platon Politeia 509b*, "Archiv für Geschichte der Philosophie" 1969, 51 , pp. 1–30. Lisi points at the lack of consequence in the interpretation by Krämer, who on the one hand presents the Good as superior to the nature, i.e. being (ἐπέκεινα τῆς οὐσίας), and on the other hand, he does not hesitate to define the One as the nature (οὐσία) of the Good itself. See F.L. Lisi, *The Foundations of Politics in the Central Books of the* Republic, [in:] *The Ascent to the Good*, ed. F.L. Lisi, Sankt Augustin 2007, p. 15. See also H.J. Krämer, *Über den Zusammenhang von Prinzipienlehre und Dialektik bei Platon. Zur Definition des Dialektikers Politeia 534b–c*, "Philologus" 1966, 110, p. 66. Let us add that in light of here presented opinion, according to which Plato ascribes to the Good a complex, twofold nature which is simultaneously directly linked to the concept of δύναμις, in the development of Plato's thought the Good should rather be conceptualized as an analogy of a pair of principles (ἕν – ἀόριστος δυάς), and not only one of them.

[36] See *Rep*. 505a.

[37] *Rep*. 517c.

[38] See *Rep*. 511b, 533a.

but only in the respect of importance and power (πρεσβείᾳ καὶ δυνάμει), thus the quoted phrase emphasizes its ultimate and not transcendental state. Therefore, the supremacy of the Good over a being is relative. The Good is more important and powerful than other ideas but it is still only an idea, and it is defined as such by Plato.

However, as it is aptly observed by Hans Georg Gadamer, in relation to the Good, Plato never refers to the word εἶδος (form) but he uses only the word ἰδέα (idea), thus emphasizing more the looking toward the Good than the look of the thing in itself, namely the Good in itself.[39] We may assume that Plato wants in this way to stress his being conscious of this specific, dialectical nature of the Good, which enforces an attempt at combining contradictory requirements: on the one hand, proving that the Good is generally cognitively available, on the other hand, showing that it is situated at the meta-level, and emphasizing its principal position.

Those two mentioned aspects, namely, the higher rank and power, due to which the nature of the Good is distinguished, really give the Good a status as αἰτία, thus they emphasize fulfilling a causative function for being. The higher rank (πρεσβείᾳ) amounts to the fact that the Good is superior to all being, since it determines the essence of an idea as an idea, and in the cognitive order, it means a logical superiority over all knowledge because it is its rationale. On the other hand, the power (δύναμις) of the Good involves being the cause of all intelligible beings and not only sensual things like in case of other ideas.[40]

Consequently, we can ascribe a threefold, causative function to the Good. In the metaphysical order, it is mediated by ideal attributes and turns out to be *causa formalis* of being,[41] whereas in the epistemological order, it is a factor activating mental intentionality of the soul for cogni-

---

[39] See H.G. Gadamer, *The Idea of the Good in Platonic-Aristotelian Philosophy*, New Haven 1988, pp. 27–28. A similar opinion is expressed by Dixsaut who thinks that Plato uses the term ἰδέα when he wants to avoid connotations related to the term εἶδος, since the latter represents definable essence of an object. See M. Dixsaut, *Platon et la question de la pensée*. Études platoniciennes I, Paris 2000, pp. 126–27. See also M. Vegetti, *op. cit.*, p. 274.

[40] See M. Dixsaut, *Métamorphoses de la dialectique dans les Dialogues de Platon*, Paris, 2001, p. 98.

[41] See *Rep.* 509b.

tive ability,[42] hence fulfilling the function of *causa cognoscendi*. On the other hand, in the practical order, the Good functions as *causa finalis* of human activity,[43] enabling self-development of man within the ethical and political order.

[42] See *Rep*. 508e.
[43] See *Rep*. 505d–e.

Anna Zhyrkova

The Academic Roots of Plotinus' Treatment of the Aristotelian Categories[1]

ABSTRACT: Plotinus' treatment of the Aristotelian categories is often presented as opposed to the Middle Platonic interpretation. Plotinus is believed to be distinct from the Middle Platonism in criticizing and rejecting the Peripatetic tradition. This approach, in my opinion, not only makes it harder to interpret Plotinus' own thought but also leads to some further difficulties, i.e. the need to explain why Aristotle's categories were re-established in the philosophical doctrine of Plotinus' pupils and successors, such as Porphyry and other Neoplatonists. I argue that Plotinus, as well as his Neoplatonic successors, formed their conceptions in the view of an established Platonic tradition of interpreting the Aristotelian doctrine of categories, which had already existed for several centuries. To prove this, I will attempt a reconstruction of the Academic and Middle Platonic interpretation of Aristotle's categories. Then, I will compare the treatment of the categories in Plotinus and in his predecessors. In my last point I will briefly refer to Porphyry's interpretation of the categories, in order to show that in spite of his differences with Plotinus, he continues and develops the Platonic tradition, which encompasses Academic, Middle Platonic and Plotinian treatments of the Aristotelian categories.

---

[1] This article is based on the paper presented at the conference of American Philosophical Association, Baltimore, December 29, 2007.

Plotinus is usually presented as a "breaking point" in the history of Platonism, that is the origin of Neoplatonism. In my opinion, however, the presentation of his doctrine separately from the previous stages of Platonism does not seem to be correct and might raise difficulties for the scholars of his work. Opposing Plotinus' treatment of the Aristotelian Categories to their Middle Platonic interpretation is one of the possible examples of this approach.

Many scholars believe that Plotinus, differs from Middle Platonism by criticizing and rejecting the Peripatetic tradition, though he shares the Medio-platonic understanding of the categories as kinds of being or existence.[2] In my opinion, such interpretation not only makes it hard to clarify Plotinus' own thought, but also leads to some further difficulties. One of them is how to explain the re-installation of the categories in the philosophical doctrine of Plotinus' pupils and successors, such as Porphyry and other Neoplatonists.[3] I argue that Plotinus and his Neoplatonic

---

[2] H.J. Blumenthal, *Plotinus in Later Platonism*, [in:] *Neoplatonism and Early Christian Thought: Essays in Honor of A.H. Armstrong*, eds. H.J. Blumenthal, R.A. Markus, London 1981, pp. 216–217.

[3] The opinion that Plotinus rejects the Aristotelian categories while his Neoplatonic successors re-install them, is accepted by many other scholars, e.g.: H.J. Blumenthal, *op. cit.*, pp. 216–217; R. Chiaradonna, *Sostanza, movimento, analogia: Plotino critico di Aristotele*, Napoli 2002; *The Categories and the Status of the Physical World: Plotinus and the Neo-platonic Commentaries*, [in:] *Philosophy, Science and Exegesis in Greek, Arabic and Latin Commentaries*, eds. P. Adamson, H. Baltussen, M.W.F. Stone, vol. 1, London 2004, pp. 121–136; C. Evangeliou, *The Ontological Basis of Plotinus' Criticism of Aristotle's Theory of Categories*, [in:] *The Structure of Being: a Neoplatonic Approach*, ed. R.B. Harris, Norfolk 1982, pp. 73–74; *Aristotle's Categories and Porphyry*, Leiden – New York 1988; A.C. Lloyd, *Neoplatonic Logic and Aristotelian Logic I*, "Phronesis" 1955, no. 1, p. 58; L.P. Gerson, *Plotinus, The Arguments of the Philosophers*, London – New York 1994, pp. 84–96. It seems that most scholars read Porphyry through the lenses of Simplicius' texts *in Cat.* 2, 5–29; 16, 16–9. The different view on the relation between categorical doctrines of Plotinus and Porphyry see P. Hadot, *The Harmony of Plotinus and Aristotle According to Porphyry*, [in:] *Aristotle Transformed: The Ancient Commentators and Their Influence*, ed. R. Sorabji, Ithaca 1990, pp. 125–140; cf. S.K. Strange, *Plotinus, Porphyry and the Neoplatonic Interpretation of the Categories*, [in:] *Aufstieg und Niedergang der Römischen Welt: Geschichte und Kultur Roms im Spiegel der neueren Forschung*, hgg. H. Temporini, W. Haase, T. 11, 36.2, Berlin – New York 1987, pp. 955–963.

successors formed their conceptions in view of an established Platonic tradition of interpreting the Aristotelian doctrine of categories, which had already existed for several centuries. In this paper, I propose a reexamination of Plotinus' treatment of Aristotle's categories in the relation to the doctrine of his Platonic predecessors. First, I will attempt a reconstruction of the Academic and Middle Platonic interpretation of Aristotle's categories. Then, I will compare the treatment of the categories in Plotinus and in his predecessors.

It is worthwhile to start the inquiry into the Platonic interpretation of the Aristotelian categories from a short description of the fundamental Academic division of reality. This division is essential for Platonic tradition and affects its treatment of the Aristotelian doctrine of categories. The first representatives of the Academy widely accepted the twofold division of reality into *Absolute* (*per se*) (καθ' αὐτό) and *Relative* being (πρός τι). To be sure, this division was ascribed to Plato by his pupil Hermodorus[4] and by Diogenes Laertius.[5] However, in Plato's text one can find only partial reminiscences on the subject.[6] In fact, the division can be traced to Xenocrates (396-314 B.C.), the third, after Plato and Speusippus, head of the Academy.[7] He recognized the principal distinction of Absolute and Relative.[8] Moreover, following Plato's *Timaeus*,[9] he distinguished two kinds of existences. The first kind corresponds to existents

[4] Hermodorus apud Simpl. *In Phys*. 248, 2ff.

[5] Diogenes Laertius in his summary of Plato's doctrine claims that it is Aristotle who ascribed to Plato the division of existing things into absolute and relative. See Diogenes Laertius, *Vitae philosophorum*, 3, 108, 7–109, 5.

[6] In the *Parmenides* a conception of πρός τι may be found; in the *Philebus* everything that exists is defined as πρός τι, and only principles are absolute; while in the *Timeaus* occurs the division into things "that always are, and into things which is becoming and never is". But *Sophist* 255C can be taken as assuming the division into Absolute and Relative. Moreover, one can find the similar division in Aristotle's doctrine too. I mean here the distinction of "being κατὰ συμβεβηκός" and "being καθ' αὐτό" which occurs in *Metaphysics* and in other places. *Metaph*. V 7, 1017a7ff. Cf. V 18, 1022a 14ff. See also *Cat*. 2a34, *An. post*. 83a25ff, etc.

[7] Sextus Empiricus, *Math*. VII 147, 1–148, 1; Xenocrates, *Testimonia, doctrina et fragmenta*, 93, 10–14; 95, 1–8.

[8] See R.E. Witt, *Albinus and the History of Middle Platonism*, Amsterdam 1971, p. 66.

[9] *Tim*. 27 d5–28a4.

sensu stricto, i.e. to ideas that are always without becoming. The second kind corresponds to existents in a week sense, i.e. to sensibles, which are becoming, but never exist. The division into Absolute and Relative, as well as the division of reality into intelligible and sensible worlds, were accepted by followers of the Academy as the fundamental dogmas and maintained with certitude.

Since Antiochus, the head of the 5th Academy, questions related to the ten categories occupied an incontestable place in the Academic philosophical discussion. The Aristotelian categories, however, were considered in relation to the Old Academic distinction regardless of the particular stance of an author to Aristotle's doctrine.[10]

The basic tenets of the Middle-platonic treatment of the categories can be found in Eudorus of Alexandria. He not only accepted the Old Academic distinction but also believed that Aristotle adopted it as well. However, he criticized the fact that Aristotle considered only the relatives and not the absolute.[11] Eudorus believed that the Aristotelian category of substance refers to sensible substances only.[12] All of the categories, thus, concern the sensible world only. And in this way they relate to the field of relatives. They are not absolute and have no relevance to the intelligible world. The next generation of the Middle-Platonists embraced the Platonic dichotomy of the Absolute and Relative being, considering the Sensible realm as the very field of the Aristotelian categories.

Plutarch, however, seems to stand out from this rule. To be sure, his treatment of the categories can hardly be reconstructed, since his *Lecture*

---

[10] Generally, one can discern two tendencies in relation to Aristotle's doctrine among the representatives of Platonic tradition: the first is characterised by an attempt of synthesis with Platonic philosophy that was due to a very strong eclectic tendency introduced to the Academy by Antiochus; the second is characterised by a hostile and critical approach to the Aristotelian doctrine. See R.E. Witt, *op. cit.*, p. 115; cf. Simplicius, *in Cat.* 30, 16; J. Dillon, *The Middle Platonists*, Ithaca 1977, p. 51. The criticism, in general, is confined to the *Categories*. Aristotle's syllogistic was not attacked. Cf. A.C. Lloyd, *op. cit.*, pp. 64–65.

[11] Simplicius, *in Cat.* 174, 14–25.

[12] Simplicius, *in Cat.* 206, 10–15.

on the Categories is not preserved,[13] while his others texts do not provide sufficient evidence. What is certain is that, whereas his predecessors ascribed the Old Academic division to Aristotle, Plutarch believed that the Aristotelian doctrine of the categories was already present in Plato's *Timaeus*.[14] Nevertheless, Plutarch's extant works contain some points that became an inspiration for further developments in the Platonic treatment of the Aristotelian categories. First of all, Plutarch returns to the *Timaeus* in setting up a much deeper contrast between the realms of Being and Becoming than his predecessors. The two realms are so different that beings belonging to Becoming have actually no part in Being. Everything that belongs to Becoming, which is the realm of the process of creation and destruction, is subject to change. And it presents only a dim and uncertain semblance and appearance of itself. Being, in opposite,

> [...] is that which is eternal, without beginning and without end, to which no length of time brings change.[15]

Secondly, Plutarch claims that in spite of its perfection even the realm of Being does not constitute an absolute unity. Instead, it differs according to its proper genera: Being, Identity, Difference (Otherness), Motion, and Rest. In other words, Plutarch proposes to the realm of Being that was earlier considered only as Absolute, the additional genera, which are in fact *megista gene* of Plato's *Sophist*.[16] What is more, he refrains from applying the Aristotelian categories to the Sensible realm. He consequently develops the idea of difference between the two realms. He assumes that the realm of Becoming is an image of the realm of Being. Consequently, the Becoming is also constituted of five elements, which are images and copies of the elements of Being. These five basic constituents of the physical world are the four elements: earth, fire, air, water; completed by the physical world as a whole.[17]

---

[13] According to the *Lamprias-Catalogue*, he wrote a work in eight books on the *Topica* and a treatise on the ten categories.

[14] Plutarch, *De animae procreatione in Timaeo*, 1023E 7–8: supra *Tim.* 37B 3- C 5. See also R.E. Witt, *op. cit.*, pp. 2–3.

[15] *E at Delphi* 391E (18)–393 A (19).

[16] Cf. *E at Delphi* 15 (B).

[17] Cf. *De def. or.* 423, 23 (A); 427, 33, (F); 428, 33 (A); 428, 34 (B–D).

The critique of the categories that was later advanced by Lucius and Nicostratus appears to be a consequence of a kind of similar view of the relation between the intelligible and sensible realms. Their critique contains almost all of the list of the main problems, with which the next generations of the Platonic commentators dealt. It is worth noticing that Simplicius, in his report of their opinions, often mentioned them next to the ones of Plotinus.

Nicostratus establishes definitively the Academic distinction as the foundation for further criticisms of the Aristotelian categories.[18] First, his analysis of the issue of to which realm the Aristotelian categories refer concludes with the claim that the ten categories contain the sensibles only. For instance, "being-affected" and "relative" cannot relate to the intelligibles, which are immutable. Therefore it appears clearly that Aristotle left the intelligibles out of his consideration.

Secondly, in relation to the genera of sensibles and intelligibles, we must deal with three following options: (1) sensibles and intelligibles have some common and some different genera; (2) the genera of sensibles and intelligibles are the same; (3) the genera of intelligibles are different from the ones of sensibles. The first option is not considered by Aristotle at all. In the second case, the categories of sensibles would be synonymous with those of intelligibles. But it is impossible, since there is no commonality between things, one of which is "prior" and the other is "posterior", and one of which is a model, the other an image. The categories, then, appear to be said of sensibles and of intelligibles homonymously. Yet, it means that the genera of two realms have in common the same name only. Thus, they are really different. Only the third option seems to be possible, the one according to which the genera of intelligibles are different from the sensibles. Consequently, we are coming to the same conclusion: the Aristotelian categories correspond to the sensibles and completely neglect the intelligibles. Moreover, there should be more genera, since the intelligibles are disregarded. This argumentation basically corresponds to the core of Plotinus' critique in the Sixth

[18] Simplicius, *in Cat.* 73, 15ff.

Ennead. Lucius and Nicostratus, then, are to be regarded as forerunners of Plotinus in this respect.[19]

The next objection raised by Nicostratus against the Aristotelian categories, which became dramatically important for the Platonists, is the problem of the unity of sensible and intelligible substances.[20] Namely, if the ten categories are regarded as referring to the Sensible realm only, then a problem arises, associated with the fact that Aristotle posits primary and secondary substance. The former typically corresponds to the sensible particulars, which might be considered as bodies, while the latter contains genera and species that are incorporeal.[21] Nicostratus, according to Simplicius' report, remarks that if something could be common to intelligible and sensible substances, it should be prior to both of them (πρὸ ἀμφοῖν ἔσται). The question of priority is here significant. Simplicius points out, in some other places, that there can be no common genus where one reality is prior and the other posterior.[22] But the intelligible substance itself is prior to the sensible one. The Aristotelian doctrine of substance, then, seems to be unacceptable under conditions that what is Intelligible is prior and is true being; whereas what is Sensible is posterior and is becoming. What is more, the common genus should be equally predicated of all its species as well as be identical with all of them. But one genus cannot be predicated equally of what is intelligible and of what is sensible. In this case, predication is homonymic only. The one common genus, obviously, cannot cover sensible, i.e. corporeal, and intelligible, i.e. incorporeal, substances, because it has to share the nature of both subjects that would

---

19 Gottschalk claims that the problem of whether the Aristotelian categories are applied to the intelligible as well as to the sensible world was already considered by Ps.- Archytas. Therefore, it is impossible to evaluate Lucius' and Nicostratus' contribution to this discussion. Gotshalk refers to Simplicius, *in Cat.* 73, 28ff, 76, 14ff; Plotinus, *Enn.* 6.1.1-2 and Simplicius, *in Cat.* 76, 19ff; 77, 8ff; ps. Archytas, *Περὶ τῶν καθολῦ λόγων*, 22, 31ff, 30, 19ff (in H. Thesleff, *The Pythagorean Texts of the Hellenistic Period*, Åbo 1965. ad loc.). See H.B. Gottshalk, *The Earliest Aristotelian Commentators*, [in:] *Aristotle Transformed: The Ancient Commentators and Their Influence*, ed. R. Sorabji, Ithaca 1990, p. 76, n. 109; p. 81, n. 138.

20 Simplicius, *in Cat.* 76.14.

21 Cf. *Cat.* 2a11–18.

22 Simplicius, *in. Cat.* 76.14; 126, 5–10; and others.

have to be neither incorporeal nor corporeal. In other words, in this case, genus would not be identifiable with one of its species. Thus, the genus of substance in its Aristotelian meaning has no generic unity. The aporia, presented above, prove to be fundamental especially for Plotinus' critique of the Aristotelian substance.[23]

For all these and many other reasons, Lucius and Nicostratus declare the ten categories of Aristotle to be insufficient and incomplete. Since the categories relate to the sensibles and neglect the intelligibles, they claim that there should be other genera related to the Intelligible realm.[24]

From all of the material reviewed until now it follows that, in the Academic tradition, the Aristotelian categories were not acknowledged as the genera of Intelligible Realm, i.e. the domain of Being, but were considered as referring to the Sensible realm only. Still, it is not clear whether they were regarded as the genera of this realm. Book VIII of Clement's *Stromata* sheds a new light on this question. All the content of this book possesses a distinctively semantic character. It is in this semantic context that Clement introduces the Aristotelian categories.

The text itself is quite problematic and deserves a separate study. In general it possible to say that Clement's account of the categories is of a rather compilatory scholastic character. In spite of that, it is significant that he discerns the categories from the genera *sensu stricto*[25] as well as from the sensible subject-things. In turn, he connects them with a kind of "elements" that are apparently identical with universals (τὰ καθόλου), according to which every subject of investigation is to be considered.[26] This seems to be one of the first signs of a new interpretation of the Aristotelian categories in the Platonic tradition. Accordingly, Clement treats the categories not as real genera of sensibles but as kinds of epistemological classes of things, according to which sensibles are considered. Therefore, the cat-

[23] Plotinus, *Enn.* VI, see below.

[24] There is even some fragmental evidence from which it follows that Lucius and Nicostratus considered the set of Aristotelian categories itself to be deficient. See Simplicius, *in Cat* 62, 29f; 64, 13–16; 66, 15.

[25] In *Str*. VIII. 6, the categories seem to be classes of species, which are different from genera of entities in the strict sense. See *Str*. VIII. 6, 20, 1, 2–3, 1; *Str*. VIII. 6, 21, 4, 1–5, 1

[26] *Str*. VIII, 8, 23, 1, 1–24, 2.

egories appear to be moved from the ontological domain to the semantic one. This resembles the Neoplatonic attempt to interpret the Aristotelian categories as related first and foremost to logic. However, it is hard to decide whether the text reflects Clement's own ideas or is just a testimony of such ideas already existing somewhere around him. In any case, it bears witness to the intellectual currency of those ideas.[27]

The complete reconstruction of the Medio-platonic treatment of the Aristotelian categories is very difficult, due to the little amount of remaining evidence and general eristic tendency of this tradition. However, it is possible to point to some general characteristics of this approach. The criticism of the Aristotelian categories, in this stage of Platonism, seems to be mainly due to the Academic vision of reality as divided into two domains of Absolute and Relative. The former constitutes the intelligible and unchangeable realm of Being; while the latter is an area of sensible and changeable things, which cannot be properly called substances or beings, but rather "coming--into-being". The realm of Being is prior to the realm of Becoming, which is only a copy or image of Absolute being. These two realms have no common genera. In this context, it is clear that the categories, of which sensible substance is the main subject, cannot relate to the domain of Absolute. The Aristotelian categories, thus, were accepted as being referred exclusively to the Relative, that is Sensible realm.

However, it is unclear whether the ten categories were considered as the genera of the Sensible realm. The categories, treated as genera applied to the sensibles, were criticized on the account of their number and order. Even if an author believed that the categories are found in Plato's works, it does not follow that he accepted them as appropriate genera for the sensibles. Instead, one can find in Middle Platonism an attempt to introduce, for the Sensible realm, the genera analogous to Plato's μέγιστα γένη, as it has occurred in Plutarch. By some others, the Aristotelian categories were treated not as genera *sensu stricto* but as universals or epistemological

[27] On account of Clement's treatment of the categories see: A. Zhyrkova, *Reconstructing Clement of Alexandria's Doctrine of Categories*, [in:] *Conversations Platonic and Neoplatonic: Intellect, Soul, and Nature: Papers from the 6th Annual Conference of the International Society for Neoplatonic Studies*, eds. R. Berchman, J. Finamore, Sankt Augustin 2010, pp. 145–154.

classes. In line with such interpretation, the categories do not appear to be in conflict with the Platonic doctrine. The idea will be developed in the further stages of the Platonic tradition.

The first of these further stages is obviously Plotinus' treatment of the Aristotelian categories. According to the generally accepted opinion, Plotinus understands the categories as corresponding to the genera of being.[28] This opinion is supported by the beginning of the text of Ennead VI.1-3 [42–44], which formed Plotinus' treatise *On the Genera of Being* (*Περὶ τῶν γενῶν τοῦ ὄντος*). However, the text does not contain such a claim. Plotinus, actually, only says that some philosophers posited the ten genera for beings.[29] He, in turn, is going to consider *whether* the well-known ten genera are to be ranged under the common name of Being (κοινοῦ ὀνόματος τυχόντα τοῦ ὄντος), or are the ten predications (κατηγορίας δέκα).[30] It seems, then, that initially he does not assume the categories to be the genera of being, but only intends to explore whether they could be interpreted in such a way.[31]

Plotinus' consideration of the categories, similarly to that of his predecessors, presupposes the fundamental Academic division of reality into the Intelligible realm of true being and the Sensible realm of becoming.[32] Consequently he accepts the opinion that the Aristotelian categories do not embrace the whole reality, namely they do not refer to intelligibles. He even claims that philosophers, who shared the tenfold division, themselves did not want to classify all beings, but omitted the most authentic beings. Plotinus seems to dwell here on the critique presented already by Nicostratus. Namely his basic argument is that there is no common genus of things among which there is priority and posteriority. Thus, the intelligibles and sensibles cannot be ranged under one and the same genus.[33]

---

[28] It is quite common opinion. See for instance L.P. Gerson, *op. cit.*, pp. 79–80; S.K. Strange, *op. cit.*, p. 22.

[29] *Enn.* VI, 1, 1, 6–10.

[30] *Enn.* VI, 1, 1, 15–18.

[31] F.A.J. De Haas, *Did Plotinus and Porphyry Disagree on Aristotle's Categories?*, "Phronesis" 2001, 44, no. 4, pp. 500–1.

[32] C. Evangeliou, *op. cit.*, p. 74.

[33] *Enn.* VI, 1, 1, 19–30.

Parallels with Nicostratus can be also found in Plotinus' treatment of the Aristotelian doctrine of substance. The substance as a genus cannot be predicated of intelligible and sensible substances synonymously. The sensible objects can be named "substance" (οὐσία) only homonymously (ὁμωνύμως).[34] The categories, according to Plotinus, do not possess generic unity, for which is required synonymy between a genus and its subject.[35] They have only the unity of common source (ἀφ' ἑνός). The Aristotelian categories, thus, are not genera in a strict sense.[36] As a matter of fact they are nothing more than κατηγορίαι – accidental (non-essential) predications and as such are opposed to the real genera.[37] In this ultimate rejection of the categories as genera Plotinus did not oppose the Middle-Platonic tradition, but rather consequently developed the interpretation of the categories, which followed from its basic principles.

Also Plotinus' doctrine of genera of being and becoming is a development of the Platonic tradition. He, like Plutarch, applies to the Intelligible Realm the genera of being (γένη τοῦ ὄντος), which correspond to the "highest kinds" (μέγιστα γένη) of Plato, namely: being (ὄν), movement (κίνησις), rest (στάσις), sameness (ταὐτόν) and difference (θάτερον).[38] However, for the sensible realm, he introduces five so-called "genera of becoming", which are different from those of Plutarch: substance (οὐσία), motion (κίνησις), quantity (ποσόν), quality (ποιόν) and relation (πρός τι).[39]

---

[34] *Enn.* VI, 3, 2, 1–4.

[35] Cf. F.A.J. De Haas, *op. cit.*, pp. 503–7.

[36] *Enn.* VI, 1, 3, 1–6.

[37] See F.A.J. De Haas, *op. cit.*, p. 513 in opposition to C. Horn, *Plotin über Sein, Zahl und Einheit: eine Studie zu den systematischen Grundlagen der Enneaden*, Stuttgart 1995, pp. 41–48. S.K. Strange, *op. cit.*, p. 69.
However, the interpretation of the categories as a kind of non-essential predications should not be taken as a support for the so-called "nominalism of sensible genera". Cf. C. Rutten, *Les catâegories du monde sensible dans les Ennâeades de Plotin*, Paris 1961, pp. 48–56; M. Isnardi Parente, *Enneadi, VI 1–3: trattati 42–44 "Sui genere dell'essere"*, Napoli 1994, p. 250.

[38] Plato *Sph.* 254a–256e.

[39] *Enn.* VI, 3, 3, 25–32. The substance is considered as matter (ὕλη), form (εἶδος) and composite (συναμφότερον).

As far as it concerns the subjects of sensible genera, Plotinus applies the Aristotelian notion of primary substance. However, he relegates the sensible substance, which is the primary substance of Aristotle's *Categories,* to the status of pseudo-substance.[40] Particular sensible substance, according to Plotinus, is always a particular *of a certain kind*. In other words it is always something qualified that is ποιὸν τί, while the real substance is the essence (τὸ τί) by itself. Plotinus claims that the sensible substance is a collection (συμφόρησις) or mixture (μίγμα) of qualities, quantities and matter.[41] In that he also follows another well-established Platonic tradition, according to which particulars appear to be a kind of collection of qualities.[42] A particular, in Plotinus' doctrine, can be interpreted rather as a logical subject than as a kind of being. It is a being only with reference to its cause. In this light, the genera of sensibles can be named genera only by analogy with the real "genera of being".[43] The sensible genera are derived from common features of sensible particular substances. The mentioned features, however, neither constitute generic unity nor reveal the real nature of the individual.[44] In other words, the sensible genera possess an accidental character. Therefore, the "genera of becoming" are nothing more than κατηγορίαι – predications, or in other words external denominations, which are ascribed to the sensible object.[45]

This account of the sensible genera presented by Plotinus in *Ennead* VI.3 [44] seems to be assumed in his treatment of Aristotle's categories

---

[40] *Enn.* VI, 2, 4, 7: οἷον οὐσία; VI, 3, 5, 1: ἐνθάδε οὐσία. Cf. J.P. Anton, *Plotinus' Approach to Categorical Theory*, [in:] *The Significance of Neoplatonism*, ed. R.B. Harris, Norfolk 1976, p. 86n; M.F. Wagner, *Plotinus on the Nature of Physical Reality*, [in:] *The Cambridge Companion to Plotinus*, ed. L.P. Gerson, Cambridge – New York 1996, p. 130.

[41] *Enn.* VI, 3, 8, 16–30.

[42] The term ἄθροισμα is found in *Theaet.* 157c; adopted by Epicurus (D.L. X, 62) and Chrysippus (SVF. II, 841). The term seems to have been also used as a technical term by Antiochus. Cf. Sextus E. *Math.* 7.276–7. It is worth mentioning that *Theaet.* 157c appears to be only a speculative theory. Plato does not apply the term ἄθροισμα to particulars, whereas for Alcinous the doctrine that a particular object is a collection of qualities is already a dogma. See *Did.* 4.7.8–12.

[43] Plotinus *Enn.* VI, 1, 1, 23–28; VI, 3, 1, 6–7; VI, 3, 2, 1–4; VI, 3, 5, 1, 2–3.

[44] Plotinus *Enn.* VI, 1, 3, 19–22.

[45] See C. Rutten, *op. cit.*, pp. 49–56. Cf. F.A.J. De Haas, *op. cit.*, pp. 507–16.

in *Ennead* VI.1 [42]. His interpretation of the sensible genera completes his criticism of the Aristotelian categories in the *Ennead* VI.1 [42]. There, Plotinus focuses on denying the status of the genera of being to the Aristotelian categories, while the analyzed text of the *Ennead* VI.3 [44] allows determining what Aristotle's categories actually are. *De facto*, they, like the sensible genera of Plotinus, are nothing more than predications.

A further development of such interpretation of the Aristotelian categories and the sensible genera is to be found in the works of Plotinus' disciple Porphyry. To be sure, Porphyry recognizes the categories as applying to the domain of sensibles,[46] but not as its genera. Despite the fact that the categories are listed according to the generic differences of things, they are not the genera by themselves.[47] The Aristotelian categories, for Porphyry, are only kinds of predication that are properly said of a subject according to each of the genera of entities.[48]

To conclude, Plotinus' treatment of the Aristotelian categories seems to be heavily dependent on the fundamental Academic distinction between Intelligible and Sensible. His critique of the Aristotelian doctrine of substance is influenced by the criticism of his predecessors, who rejected the generic unity of the Aristotelian substance on the basis of relations of priority/posteriority and being original/image of intelligible and sensible substances respectively. Plotinus does not reject the Middle-Platonic interpretation of the categories, but rather consequently develops it according to Platonic principles. As a result, he treats the categories (as well as sensible genera) as quasi-genera or kinds of predications. The same approach will be developed by his Neoplatonic successors. Therefore, it is possible to say that there is one consistently developed tradition of interpretation of the categories, which encompasses Academic, Middle Platonic and Neoplatonic doctrines.

---

[46] Porphyrius *in Cat.* 91, 7.

[47] See Porphyrius *in Cat.* 58, 6–15; 70, 29–33; 71, 11–14; 19–26.

[48] Porphyrius *in Cat.* 57, 20–29; 59, 20–33.

Rafał Oleś

The Highest Genera of Being and Substantial Unity in Plotinus' Ontology

ABSTRACT: The subject of this article is a generic analysis of being in Plotinus' ontology. We aim to explore the structure of the noetic Cosmos (κόσμος νοητός) and Intellect (νοῦς) from the perspective of the highest genera and to expose the formal and ontological attributes of the highest genera as well as to investigate their inter-dependences and the form of unity which these genera create together – called here a substantial unity. In the first part of the article, we will demonstrate the relation between the genera constituting the lower ontic levels (the nature of body and soul) and the type of the constituted unity. In the second part, the concept of Being will be compared with other concepts (such as: Quality, Good, Beauty and One) employed by Plotinus in the generic analysis presented mainly in Enn. VI. 2 [43]. This comparison will result in a formal and ontological characteristics of the highest genera. In the third part, we will demonstrate that the unity co-constituted by the highest genera is the noetic transparency and self-transparency.

The aim of the article is to present the generic analytics of being in Plotinus' ontology and in particular to elicit the most important attributes defining what the highest genera (μέγιστα γένη) are as such, and to discuss the character of their interdependence and the form of unity related therewith.

The generic analytics in Plotinus comprises two ontic domains: the noetic cosmos (κόσμος νοητός) and the sensible cosmos (κόσμος αἰσθητός)[1] – its purpose is to elicit the immanent relation between genera and the substantial unity[2] connected with them, characteristic of the specific ontic domain. The notion of substance in the strict sense refers to Intellect (νοῦς) and secondarily to soul (ψυχή). Substance in a broader and ambiguous meaning also comprises the nature of body which, with regard to its ontic imperfection, is called by Plotinus *quasi-substance.*[3] In general, genera of being are understood as principles (ἀρχαί) which account for "completion" of the examined type of substance. The mode wherein this "establishing" of completion or perfection occurs is variously instantiated in accordance with the ontic domain wherewith the examined type of substance is related.[4]

---

[1] From the beginning of considerations on genera of being – i.e. from *Enn.* VI. 1 [42] – Plotinus highlights the contrast between the noetic sphere and the sensible order. It is also bound up with the difference of metaphysical status of genera – it is obvious that genera of noetic sphere are μέγιστα γένη in the strict sense because they are genera of being qua being and not being qua imitation of being. This metaphysical duplication κόσμος αἰσθητός does not release us, however, from the ontological examination of generic endowment of this dimension. On the distinct – in pursuance of the ontic level – comprehension of genera, see A. Woszczyk, *Podstawy Plotyńskiej krytyki teorii kategorii Arystotelesa,* "Folia Philosophica" 2011, vol. 29, pp. 172–173.

[2] "Substantial unity" is not a technical notion of Plotinus, I use it as a heuristic notion which comprises all ontic levels and it means the mutual completion of genera of a specific type of substance.

[3] In the tractate devoted to the genera of the sensible domain Plotnus writes that the nature of body *Enn.* VI. 3 [44]. 2. 3–4: "[…] should not properly be called substance at all but coming into being (γένεσιν), because it is adapted to the idea of things in flux". Plotinus, *Enneads*, trans. by A.H. Armstrong, vol. VI, London 1988, p. 181.

[4] The genera of a given order of being are the genera which determine the structure of each specific substance belonging to a given ontic order, hence one can speak of the genera

In the first part of the article I will deal with those excerpts of *Enn.* VI. 2 [43] whose aim was to prepare the appropriate analyses concerning μέγιστα γένη and which undertook the problem of generic interdependence (origins) in connection with the bodily substance and soul. Then I will pass on to the generic analytics of substance in the strict sense, i.e. noetic substance as such.

Generic analytics of nature of body and soul

In *Enn.* VI. 2 [43]. 4. 1–13 the first analysis of the substantial unity is undertaken and it concerns the nature of body and its generic unity:

> If we wanted to see the nature of body (τὴν σώματος φύσιν), [and asked ourselves] something like what nature of body itself was in this [perceptible] universe, when we had got to know thoroughly in the case of one of its parts – a stone for instance – that there was what functioned as its substrate (ὑποκείμενον), and its quantity, the magnitude, and its quality, colour for instance, should we not say in the case of every other body that there was what might be called substance (οὐσία), and quantity (ποσόν), and quality (ποιόν), all together, but divided by our reasoning into three (τῷ δὲ λόγῳ διαιρεθέντα εἰς τρία), and that body was the three as one? But if it also had movement as a natural part of its constitution, and we counted this in as well, then the four also would be brought to completion (τὸ ἓν ἀπήρτιστο) by them all in respect of its unity and its own nature.[5]

Genera[6] (here: substrate, quantity, quality, movement) constitute here the completion (τὸ ἓν ἀπήρτιστο) and the unity, specific to the bodily nature. How to understand, however, this unity of the nature of body which

---

of being as origins (principles) of substance as well as the ontic domain where to belong particular substances.

[5] Plotinus, *op. cit.*, pp. 121–123.

[6] In the quoted passage Plotinus does not call the abovementioned ontological characteristics (i.e. subject, quality, quantity, movement) genera, because he will deal with this issue more strictly not until the tractate VI.3.[43] – which I will not discuss in the article.

is mutually brought to completion by all genera? One may infer from the above that it cannot be the conceptual unity of, so to speak, a model which consists of functionally complementary "parameters" (here identical with genera), since Plotinus claiming that all genera are together, "but divided by our reasoning into three" – emphasizes that it is the pre-conceptual unity. It cannot be the unity of the actual body either because each particular body already has specific qualities, specific quantity, specific movement – thereby constitutes the specific sensible substance – and this divides "to infinity" – which is implied in the excerpt of *Enn.* VI. 2 [43]. 4. 19–22:

> [...] for the same one [can be divided] to infinity, and its colour (τὸ χρῶμα) is different from its shape (τὸ σχῆμα); for they are in fact separated (χωρίζεται).[7]

In case of a unitary sensible substance not only our notions divide it into the multitude of genera and forms but it is also supplemented by the spatial divisibility: this type of separation is perceptible above all in "understanding through sense-perception" (τὴν δι' αἰσθήσεως κατανόησιν).[8] Nevertheless, the sensible substance does not have in itself – as the sensible substance – the basis for its unity; the unity of a particular body is consolidated in the generic unity of nature of body, which in turn belongs to another ontological order of a higher form of unity – which is shown in the excerpt of *Enn.* VI. 2 [43]. 5. 8–10:

> [...] since, then, they [bodies] are from a one, but not a one such as to be in every way one or the absolute One – for this would not have made a discrete plurality – it remains that they must be from a plurality which is one. But what made them is soul: this then is a plurality which is one.[9]

The fact is, however, that in later considerations the notion of genus will be used also in reference to the sensible domain.

[7] Plotinus, *op. cit.*, p. 123.

[8] See *Enn.* VI. 3 [44]. 4. 15; Plotinus, *op. cit.*, p. 123.

[9] See *Enn.* VI. 3 [44]. 4. 15; Plotinus, *op. cit.*, p. 125.

The aforementioned "higher form of unity" cannot be the absolute One, because between the One and the Many organised in the One (particular sensible substances) must occur intermediate forms determined by the ratio of one to many. This intermediate one-many is soul (ψυχή).

It's worth noting that the World-Soul, despite the fact that it is a separate hypostasis (versus the One and Intellect) does not constitute the ontic domain of a separate generic constitution versus Intellect (νοῦς) – it is merely an example of the particular substance which pertains to the noetic ontic domain[10]. In other words, from the metaphysical perspective the soul is hypostasis (ὑπόστασις) and in this sense it constitutes an autonomous sphere, whereas in the ontological approach it pertains to the noetic ontic domain of an adequate generic profile.[11] Therefore, the analyses of "origins" (principles) of the soul (ψυχή) as a specific noetic substance,[12] are supposed to bring us closer to the highest genera of being *sensu stricto*.

Soul is one-many in two ways: on the one hand it is a multitude of rational principles, because in the mode of activity it is what causes and organizes what is "other" – in this aspect the soul's substance constitutes the unity of principles as their power (δύναμις) and "hub" (κεφάλαιον); on the other hand it is one-many in itself just as a substance. Bearing in mind that we are interested in the substantial unity as such, in the following part I will focus on the latter form of one-many, typical of soul whereon the first form – soul as power of rational principles – is dependent. Therefore, I will pass on to the generic analysis of substantial unity of soul which Plotinus begins from undertaking the problem of rela-

[10] Which is rendered by the following statement (*Enn.* VI. 2 [43]. 4. 29–30; Plotinus, *op. cit.*, p. 125): "Since, then, this soul has come ready to hand for us from the »intelligible place« (τοῦ νοητοῦ τόπου)".

[11] If soul (ψυχή) generically does not differ from Intellect (νοῦς) and also the vertical gradation occurs in it (qua hypostasis) and thereby the possibility of "movement downward" and the possibility of "temporalization" of its activity, thence one may draw the hypothesis that within its confines there is a tendency to overemphasize the aspect of difference and movement versus Intellect (νοῦς).

[12] This ontological affinity of the soul qua ὑπόστασις to the noetic sphere is even more distinctly apparent when Plotnus grasps soul as genus or division (*Enn.* VI. 2 [43]. 22. 28–29; Plotinus, *op. cit.*, p. 175): "And since Soul acts as genus (γένος) or specific form (εἶδος), the other souls act as specific forms (εἴδη)".

tion between "existence" of soul and its other powers – this is the relevant excerpt (*Enn.* VI. 2 [43]. 5. 18–27):

> For everyone would agree that the soul exists (εἶναι): but is this really the same thing as saying that a stone exists? Certainly not. But all the same there in the case of the stone also, existing (τὸ εἶναι) for the stone is not [just] being but being a stone (τὸ λίθῳ εἶναι); so here, existing for soul has being soul along with being (τὸ ψυχῇ εἶναι). Is then being (εἶναι) one thing, and the rest something else, which contributes to the completion of the substance of the soul (ὅ σθμπλεροῖ τὴν τῆς ψυχῆς οὐσίαν) and is there being [as such] (τὸ ὄν) and an essential difference (διαφορά) makes the soul? No, the soul is a particular being (τι ὄν) but not in the way that a man is white (ἄνθρωπος λευκός), but only and simply like a particular substance (οὐσία μόνον); and this is the same as saying that it does not have what it has from outside its substance (τῷ μὴ ἔξωθεν τῆς οὐσίας ἔχειν ὃ ἔχει).[13]

Plotinus asks here about the relation between "being" (εἶναι) and something which completes the substantial unity of soul; the philosopher, while indicating the difference between the expression "a man is white" and the completion of the substance, claims that the completion is not here merely something "external" in relation to the substance itself, that is a quality (as it is with whiteness inherent to man); we shall see in the following part that the relation between "completion", quality and substance is more complex in Plotinus' ontology. At this moment the essential fact is that the property "making" soul what it is, pertains to its substance and it is its immanent power. What are other powers of soul? First of all movement and thinking (contemplation). Plotinus writes about the relationship between being and life in soul in the excerpt of *Enn.* VI. 2 [43]. 6. 5–9:

> Then what will existence (τὸ εἶναι) be to it, without all the rest, different from a stone? Now this being of soul (τὸ εἶναι αὐτῆς ἐντός) must be within, like a "source and principle" (πηγὴν

[13] Plotinus, *op. cit.*, p. 127.

> καὶ ἀρχήν), or rather must be all that it is; so it must be life; and both must be one, being and life (τὸ εἶναι καὶ τήν ζωήν).[14]

Why "existence" (τὸ εἶναι) of soul grasped without "all the rest" (ἄνεθ τῶν ἄλλων) is only a body ("stone")? Body as such *exists* but it does not have actual life, whereas it does not have actual being from itself either. Body is not only the imitation of being but it is also a "shadow" of life and thought. It seems that Plotinus while saying τὸ εἶναι bears in mind a broader meaning including whatever, something which is somehow, i.e. even something which is devoid of other, let's call it "metaphysical values" such as life and thinking. To say it out: "exist" of soul without "all the rest" is being something soulless, that is body. From the above one may advance the thesis that "exist" has here a wider range than life and thought: such application of τὸ εἶναι, however, rare in Plotinus – usually a privation of life and thoughts is also a privation of being; to grasp it strictly, i.e. from the perspective of criteria applied by Plotinus himself the term "exist" in the above usage does not constitute a generic definition because it comprises apart from something which is "always being" also what is merely becoming ("image" of true being). The above analyses imply that "exist" without "all the rest" is not pure "exist" in the existential meaning (without any definition) because it concerns what is becoming and it is the sensible substance. In the generic analysis of substance-as-such, which Plotinus will conduct in the following part, we shall see that being qua genus which constitutes substance-as-such cannot be thought without the metaphysical values such as life and thought complementing its perfection. Negating in soul those two latter "components" would be identical with degrading it to the level of what imitates being, if not to matter.

Further, emphasizing the fact that "exist" of soul is related to its "source and principle", it will suggest that what actually accounts for soul is something immanent for it – unlike quality (e.g. whiteness inherent to man) whose formal quality is "externality".

---

[14] Plotinus, *op. cit.*, pp. 127–129.

As long as bodies of the generic characteristics were "edified", above all, by senses, then in case of soul the relation between the substantial unity and the genera constituting it, is given in self-contemplation; this contemplation also pertains to the substance of soul, since it is in thought that soul reveals itself as the multitude of powers – which is rendered in the excerpt of *Enn.* VI. 2 [43]. 6. 18–20:

> And its contemplation (θεωρία) is the cause (αἰτία) of its appearing many, that it may think: for if it appears as one, it did not think, but is that One.[15]

In the passage above, one can see the parallelism of *ordo essendi* and *ordo cognoscendi*. Contemplation – as something whereby soul reveals itself its generic complexity – is contained in the structure of soul and it is the movement (qua life) of establishing itself as multitude through soul; if the movement of self-contemplation was not possible it would mean that ψυχή is solely the One.

The aim of deliberations over the generic structure of soul was the introduction to the generic analytics κόσμος νοητός; such a transition is feasible for the reason that soul exemplifies here the noetic substance and as such is the specific noetic substance.[16] In the next part, where Plotinus will reflect on the highest genera as roots of substance as such, we will be able to instantiate something which accounts for the unity of genera of a given ontic domain and not only – as hitherto – consider them on the ground of a certain specific substance. However, before I will pass on to the outline of what this unity of genera of substance as such consists in, it will be worthwhile to take a look at the formal-ontological[17] characteristics of the highest genera, which may be elicited from the tractate VI.2.

---

[15] See *Enn.* VI. 2 [43]; Plotinus, *op. cit.*, p. 129.

[16] See the footnotes 10 and 12.

[17] Speaking about the formal characteristics of genera I mean such definitions of them which – at least postulatively – cannot be comprehended as genera or ideas because they would be the "successive" highest genera whose priority should again be substantiated mentioning the distinctive factors which again could be comprehended as the highest genera, etc. – we would expose ourselves then to *regressus ad infinitum*. On the other hand, the status of these definitions should be somehow substantiated from within the system, however this is not the aim of the article, therefore – for the sake of

The formal attributes of the highest genera

In this part of the article, the notion of genus will be juxtaposed with other notions which are applied by Plotnus in the generic analytics, mainly presented in *Enn.* VI. 2 [43]. The purpose of this juxtaposition is eliciting the formal-ontological characteristics of the highest genera.

1. Genus versus substance and ideas

The most essential features of the highest genera are being a root, *resp.* the principle of substance and comprising eidetic divisions. In *Enn.* VI. 2 [43]. 2. 10–17 Plotinus writes:

> If this is so, these must certainly not only be genera but at the same time also principles of being (ἀρχὰς τοῦ ὄντος ἅμα ὑπάρχειν): genera, because there are other lesser genera under them and subsequently species and individuals; principles, if being is thus composed of many and the whole derives its existence (τὸ ὅλον ὑπάρχει) from these. If then there were a number of originative constituents and they came together as wholes and made the all while having nothing else subordinated to them, they would be principles, but not genera.[18]

What does being the principle of being consist in? We have already encountered this attribute at the analysis of the substance of soul. The thing is that generic definitions are immanent for substance, and in this boundary instance, for substance as such, i.e. they are the genera "defining" being something in general. But if they were roots in the ordinary sense, they would "lose themselves"[19] in the mixture of the whole – this type of mixture ontologically pertains to κόσμος αἰσθητός thus to high-

---

the analyses hereby – I will use the definition "formal characteristics", bearing in mind the externality of those definitions with respect to the highest genera themselves (i.e. externality to being, identity, difference, rest and movement).

[18] Plotinus, *op. cit.*, p. 115.

[19] Plotinus writes in VI. 2 [43]. 2. 22–23: "But then each and every thing will be potential and not actual, and each will not be itself in a pure state". Plotinus, *op. cit.*, p. 115.

light the difference between the mixture of material roots and the whole created by "noetic roots" Plotinus must introduce the additional feature of the latter and it is actually being such a communion and whole including what is different (minor genera, divisions and individuals), which concurrently allows to retain their purity. So it must be the noetic whole, i.e. the whole whose "parts" are not separate, since they are non-material but different.

2. Genus versus the One[20]

Plotinus states that the pure One – i.e. unconnected with being – cannot be predicated on anything[21] thus obviously cannot be a genus. The One not concatenated with being, that is not the one which is predicated on being, while saying that being is oneness qua one-many, is "undifferentiated",[22] consequently it cannot have any subgenera or subspecies. The assumption of the possibility of dividing and the possibility of possessing eidetic divisions – necessary for being the highest genus – is correct only in relation to something which is already a multitude.

Each genus is distinguished by the fact that if it is truly predicated then its antithesis cannot be predicated of the same. While each eidetic division and subgenus whereof the genus is predicated is the one and the many, the one cannot be a genus. If the unity characteristic of genus is not a genus itself so what it actually is? Plotinus instantiates it as "whole in many" (πολλοῖς ὅλον).[23]

The next important remark regarding the formal characteristics of the highest genera is included by Plotinus in the following statement (*Enn.* VI. 2 [43]. 10. 32–33.):

---

[20] The present analysis includes the following chapters: *Enn.* VI. 2 [43]. 9–12.

[21] It is worthy of note that in the tractate VI. 9. Plotinus makes the opposite assumption.

[22] In *Enn.* VI. 2 [43]. 9. 9 Plotinus writes: "Again, if it is undifferentiated [The One] in itself how could it make specific forms?". Plotinus, *op. cit.*, p. 139.

[23] Plotinus writes thereon in *Enn.* VI. 2 [43]. 12. 12–14: "No, the generic one is like a whole in many (πολλοῖς ὅλον) things. Does it exist only in the things which participate in it? No, but it exists both independently and in the things which participate in it". Plotinus, *op. cit.*, p. 151.

> Now, first of all it is not necessary, if something exists in many things, that it should be a genus, either of the things in which it exists or of other things[24]

– existing in many things is sine qua non of being a genus but it is not a sufficient condition because – as the philosopher claims in *Enn.* VI. 2 [43]. 10. 38–40 – the community typical of genus

> [...] must employ differentiations which belong to itself and make specific forms and make them in its essential being.[25]

To conclude the argument, Plotinus points out that the One cannot be complex, it cannot be something later in relation to something else, whereas being can unite with any segment of opposites: *prior – posterior, simple – composite.*[26] Certainly such distinctions as *prior – posterior* concern here divisions of being, that is particular beings, i.e. some beings are simple and other composite and thereby they differentiate being internally – therefore they may be treated as vertical differences between ideas.[27] But do they refer to being qua genus? Since Plotinus admits that the highest genera are "primary" genera in relation to other, then why they (mentioned opposites: *prior – posterior, simple – composite*) do not belong to the highest genera beside identity, difference, movement, rest? It appears that Plotinus will undertake this issue not until the treatise dedicated to numbers.

3. Genus versus quality[28]

At the beginning of *Enn.* VI. 2 [43]. 4 Plotinus maintains that the primary substance cannot consist of qualities and whereby "approach its completion" because substance cannot be subsequent to quality. At first sight

---

[24] Plotinus, *op. cit.*, p. 145.

[25] See *Enn.* VI. 2 [43]. 12. 12–14; Plotinus, *op. cit.*, p. 145.

[26] See Plotinus, *op. cit.*, p. 151.

[27] *Prior – posterior* and *simple – composite* cannot be the horizontal differences since genus is predicated unequivocally on divisions and to an equal degree constitutes the "core" of all the ideas pertaining to a given genus. See Plotinus, *op. cit.*, p. 91.

[28] The present analysis comprises the chapters: *Enn.* VI. 2 [43]. 14–15.

this statement is not so obvious, especially as in the tractate VI. 3 [44]. 8. 30–37 Plotinus does not see any problem in the approach of the sensible substance as "bundle of qualities" (that is from "non-substance"). It will become clear after eliciting the formal ontological characteristics of something which Plotinus calls here "quality" and "completion". Within the framework of this analysis we will be able to confront the formal attributes of quality with the requirements imposed by Plotinus on the highest genera.

Plotinus distinguishes substance as such from specific substances referring to the differentiation: *simple – composite*; substance as such cannot be completed by something which is complex because it conditions specific substances and what constitutes the condition, cause or principle of something else must be simpler in its ontic structure. In *Enn.* VI. 2 [43]. 14. 5–14 the philosopher writes:

> In composite substances, then, which are made up of many elements, and in which numbers and quantities produce their differentiation, there might also be qualities, and a certain common element will be discerned in them; but in the primary genera the distinction which must be made is not between simples and composites but between simples and those which make an essential contribution to substance, not to a particular substance.[29]

In the further part of the treatise it turns out that the highest genera cannot be also called "completions" of substance as such (οὐσίας ὅλως) because it implies that the substance does not have them "from itself". Thanks to the above distinctions the thing may be arranged as follows:

1. Substance as such – is solely the highest genera in their unity; genera are neither completions nor qualities though they are activities of substance as such.[30]

---

[29] See *Enn.* VI. 2 [43]. 12. 12–14; Plotinus, *op. cit.*, p. 155.

[30] Whereof Plotinus writes in *Enn.* VI. 2 [43]. 15. 6–10: "For if movement is the activity of substance, and being and the primary genera altogether are actively actual, movement could not be something incidental, but, being the activity of what is actively actual, could not any longer be called something which contributes to the completion of substance [...]". Plotinus, *op. cit.*, p. 157.

2. Specific noetic substance[31] – has essential qualities which are activities of specific substance but they are not activities of substance as such. In this case "completion", "activity" and "quality" prove interchangeable.[32]
3. Particular sensible substance – consists of the qualities which are not activities but only passive affections.

In other words, sensible quality is constituted in the "passive affection" whose substrate is matter and what acts is substance qua specific noetic substance; the noetic quality is both completion and the activity of substance qua specific noetic substance; the highest genera which account for substance as such are neither qualities in the sense of completion nor qualities in the sense of a passive affection – nevertheless they are activities.[33]

---

[31] Specific substance is comprehended here as a rational form (λόγοι) – above all in the sense of being solely "something" which is contrasted with being "something like". In another place Plotinus writes *Enn.* VI. 3 [44]. 15. 24–31: "It was said about the qualitative that, mixed together with others, matter and the quantitative, it effects the completion of sensible substance, and that this so-called substance is this compound of many, and is not a »something« but a »something like«; and the rational form, of fire for instance, indicates rather the »something«, but the shape it produces is rather a quale. And the rational form of man is the being a »something«, but its product in the nature of body, being an image of the form, is rather a sort of »something like«". Plotinus, *op. cit.*, p. 225.

[32] Whereof Plotinus writes in *Enn.* VI. 2 [43]. 14. 14–19: "All the same, we did think it right to say elsewhere that the elements which contributed to the essential completion of substance were qualities only in name, but those which came from outside subsequent to substance were qualities [in the proper sense], and that those which were in substances were their activities, but those which came after them were already passive affections. But now we are saying that the elements of particular substance make no contribution at all to the completion of substance as such (οὐσίας ὅλος)". Plotinus, *op. cit.*, p. 155.

[33] Thanks to the distinctions made, the problem of quality may be put in order:
a) Noetic quality – is activity and completion of specific substance. Whereas completion means here the necessary component for being something which substance is as such specific substance.
b) Sensible quality – is "passive affection" of matter and completion of sensible substance.

To recapitulate the above deliberations, one can claim that the formal attribute of quality is internality to something whose completion it is: sensible quality is internal to particular sensible substance, noetic quality is internal to specific noetic substance; another formal attribute of quality is externality to something which accounts for the cause of something whose completion quality is; the cause of sensible substance is noetic substance, hence sensible quality is external to noetic substance; substance as such is the cause[34] of specific noetic substance, hence noetic quality is external to substance as such. The latter also prompts why genera cannot be contribution to the completion of substance as such: being completion and being activity are formally already inherent to noetic quality;[35] if genera were completions they should be identified with noetic qualities (genera would fulfil their formal-ontological attributes). Thus genera are merely activities of substance but they do not contribute to its "completion".

Thanks to the above distinctions we know what formal attributes are inherent to the genus as a primary genus: it is neither quality in the sense of a passive affection nor quality in the sense of completion – however it is activity (ἐνέργεια).[36]

4. Genus versus the good and the beauty[37]

In *Enn.* VI. 2 [43].17. 20–21 Plotinus substantiates that, assuming that the "good" or the beauty is a genus, we cannot state that it is the highest genus:

> […] for a thing's being good is posterior to its being and its being something, even if it always accompanies them, but those

---

[34] The notion of cause in this case would require instantiation or perhaps even replacing with another notion; however it seems that in this place it is enough to refer to the neoplatonic principle that whole "precedes" parts – in this sense substance as such conditions specific substance.

[35] See the footnote 33.

[36] See F.A.J. de Haas, *Did Plotinus and Porphyry Disagree on Aristotle's "Categories"?* "Phronesis" 2001, vol. 4, p. 514; A.C. Lloyd, *The Anatomy of Neoplatonism*, Oxford 1991, pp. 85–95; A. Woszczyk, *op. cit.*, p. 173.

[37] At this point I refer to some considerations included in *Enn.* VI. 2 [43]. 17.

> [primary genera] belong to being as being (τοῦ ὄντος ᾗ ὄν) and enter into substance.[38]

From the quoted passage one can draw the next formal ontological feature of the highest genus: while being the genus of being qua being (τοῦ ὄντος ᾗ ὄν) it is the genus of being qua substance (one-many) and something that something is what it is.

5. Summary: The elicited formal-ontological attributes of genus

The highest genera must be the genera of *being qua being* that is: they must be immanent for substance as its *activities*. Genus must be *pure* and *simple* and also *be connected* with other genera, it must "cause" differentiations and divisions, to be *immanently differentiated* – in other words it must be *whole in many*; as Ch. Evangeliou[39] remarks, genera while being *numerically different* (single) they are actually *identical in nature* – it results from the fact that substance is not something different from genera since, as already mentioned, they are its activities.

The highest genera of being qua being

What genera meet the above requirements? They are the genera known from the dialogue *Sophist* by Plato: being, movement, rest, identity and difference. Certainly the question arises: how those genera meet the above formal attributes? Most descriptions concerning μέγιστα γένη in *Enn.* VI. 2 [43] aim at showing "interactivity" of genera, exhibiting their primordial unity in substance. Therefore, I return to the problem raised at the beginning of this article, i.e. characterising of the substantial unity νοῦς "constituted" by the highest genera. What metaphysical character does this one-many have in νοῦς? It is worth adducing here William R. Inge's remark:

---

[38] Plotinus, *op. cit.*, p. 161.

[39] Ch. Evangeliou, *Aritotel's Categories and Porphyry*, Leiden 1996, p. 132.

> The whole theory of categories is open to criticism. Proclus supports my contention that Plotinus would have done better to discard the Platonic and Aristotelian lists, and to make Goodness, Truth, and Beauty the attributes of Spirit and its world. It would then be clear that the Spiritual World is a Kingdom of Values, Values of truly existing Reality. Goodness, Truth, and Beauty are in our experience ultimates. They cannot be fused, or wholly harmonised, but they have the characteristic of mutual inclusion which belongs to the Spiritual World.[40]

This what is metaphysical and in the aggregate characterises κόσμος νοητός is actually the mutual inclusion and illumination of all ("the characteristic of mutual inclusion") – and it is difficult not to agree with that part of W.R. Inge's statement. However, do not the highest genera (being, identity, difference, movement, rest) really give this metaphysical specificity of the noetic sphere? It appears that the highest genera are capable of grasping both as components of each idea separately[41] but also, and perhaps above all, as aspects of substance[42] they account for what may be called immanent transparency of νοῦς. What is this "transparency"?

The highest genera as certain forms must be the objects of intellect.[43] But the objects of intellect are not outside the intellect, they must be what it is itself, and since they are "primary" genera they must be νοῦς in the "prime" mode. Thus primary genera are νοῦς not only in the sense of immanent self-differentiation like ideas but they are such whereby this contemplation of beings in νοῦς occurs, that is this remaining in itself and differentiation,[44]

---

[40] W.R. Inge, *The Philosophy of Plotinus*, vol. II, London 1918, s. vii.

[41] Plotinus writes about that function of genera in *Enn.* VI. 2 [43]. 8. 25–28: "So all things are being, rest and motion; these are all-pervading genera, and each subsequent thing is a particular being, a particular rest, and a particular motion". Plotinus, *op. cit.*, p. 135.

[42] See A.H. Armstrong, *An Introduction to Ancient Philosophy*, London 1965, p. 247.

[43] It is particularly noticeable while considering being, rest and movement in *Enn.* VI. 2 [43]. 8. 1–3: "But one must posit these three, if Intellect thinks each of them separately; but it does at once know and posit them, if it thinks, and they exist, if they have been thought". Plotinus, *op. cit.*, p. 133.

[44] Plotnus writes in *Enn.* VI. 2 [43]. 8. 7–9: "You see the hearth of substance and a sleepless light on it, and how they stand on it and how they stand apart, existing all together". Plotinus, *op. cit.*, p. 133.

i.e. it is in itself qua subject whereas qua object it is in the other; *being* is subject through *thinking* and thinking is already *movement*, i.e. the activity proceeding from being (immanent self-transcendence of being through its activity), therefore formally the activity of establishing object is self-negation of being but – as it is *pure thought* which is true in essence and so it is itself its object[45] – it must think being itself and must be being, hence self-negation of being is the immanent negation (intra-ontic negation), the negation determined through the relationship between subject and object, negation of being (qua subject) in being (qua object) and *vice versa*, that is *difference* ("indeterminate" negation would be separation); thus intellect "reveals itself" to itself in object again qua being, however it is being in *modi* of immanent difference, so it differentiates itself in object to multitude of eidetic beings. Every idea, for it is being, does not originate or disappear, thus it is truly being – which is its sustainability and eternity, that is *rest*.[46] Each idea qua essence is *self-identical*, i.e. it is "determinate something", it is complete and finite in itself (i.e. "finished"). The difference between self-identical beings is their mutual negation but it is the determinate negation – in this connection "why" of a given idea is included in "relations" of ideas to other ideas, that is to νοῦς (just like particular parts of knowledge acquire their complete sense and significance thanks to relations to other, determinate and complete in itself parts of knowledge, and thereby to the whole), hence every idea is an intelligible one-many because each has in itself all other ideas as constituting its rationale;[47] in this connection vision of ideas is the

[45] In *Enn*. VI. 2 [43]. 8. 4–5 Plotinus writes: "[…] things which are without matter have been thought, this is their being". Plotinus, *op. cit.*, p. 133.

[46] See Plotinus, *op. cit.*, p. 131.

[47] In *Enn*. VI. 7 [38]. 1. 54–58 Plotinus writes: "All things, then, existed already and existed for ever, and existed in such a way that one could say later »this after that«; for when it is extended and in a sense unfolded it is able to display this after that, but when it is all together it is entirely this; but this means having its cause also in itself". Plotinus, *op. cit.*, vol. VII, p. 89. For a more complete depiction of the issue of relation between idea and causality, see W.R. Emilson, *Plotinus on Intellect*, New York 2007, p. 200; K. Corrigan, *Essence and Existence in "Enneads"*, [in:] *The Cambridge Companion to Plotinus*, ed. L.P. Gerson, Cambridge 1996, pp. 110–112; M.F. Wagner, *op. cit.*, p. 158.

vision of all intelligible "relations" which account for what it is, but in the manner that it is itself this self-sufficient whole[48] – i.e. the whole of these relations to other ideas is it itself as its "why" (reason). Yet how is it possible? Everything that is in νοῦς is νοῦς, thus each idea as νοῦς has in its power all other ideas and owing to that a given idea as such is identical with its "why"[49]. The above implies that while "seeing" an idea we see its "intelligibility", that is its "why" being it as νοῦς.[50] Therefore, νοῦς always "discovers" itself in the object of thinking, since it "makes itself being and being itself",[51] and in this sense νοῦς is identical with its object, for knowledge of things without matter is its objects. Hence νοῦς as the essence of truth is self-transparent:

> [...] it [νοῦς] will need no proof and no confirmation that it is so [...] and is manifest to itself [...] and nobody can confirm this about it better than itself – and it knows clearly that all this is there in the intelligible world, and really there[52].

The highest genera – qua moments (aspects) of this immanently differentiated dynamics of permeation of νοῦς and ideas – exhibit Intellect as self-transparent nature, that is the essence of truth and allow to "instill" the intuition of one-many which is the second hypostasis. In conclusion it is worth recalling the excerpt of *Enn.* V. 8 [31]. 4. 1–7 which may present the synthesis of the above analyses of νοῦς:

---

[48] This dialectical coupling of rationale (reasons) is perfectly reflected in the following passage of *Enn.* VI. 7 [38]. 2. 38–44: "If therefore there is a joint existence of all things together, of all things with nothing random about it, and there must be no separation, then the things caused would have their causes in themselves, and each would be of such a kind as possess its cause causelessly. If then the intelligibles have no cause of their being but are selfsufficent and independent of cause, they would be in possession of their cause in themselves and with themselves". Plotinus, *op. cit.*, vol. VII, pp. 91–93.

[49] Plotinus writes about that identity in *Enn.* VI. 7 [38]. 2. 10–11.

[50] Which is rendered in the excerpt of *Enn.* VI. 5 [23]. 6. 1–4: "For the intelligibles are many and they are one, and, being one, they are many by their unbounded nature, and many in one and one over many and all together, and they are active towards the whole with the whole, and active towards the part again with the whole". Plotinus, *op. cit.*, vol. VI, p. 339.

[51] *Enn.* VI. 2 [43]. 8. 18, p. 135.

[52] *Enn.* V. 5 [32]. 2. 13–18, p. 175.

For it is "the easy life" there, and truth in their mother and nurse and being and food – and they see all things (καὶ ὁρῶσι τὰ πάντα), not those to which coming to be, but those to which real being belongs, and they see themselves in other things; for all things there are transparent (ἀλλὰ πᾶς παντὶ φανερὸς εἰς τὸ εἴσω), and there is nothing dark or opaque [...], for light is transparent to light (φῶς γὰρ φωτί) [...].[53]

[53] *Enn*. V. 8 [31]. 4. 1–6, pp. 248–249.

Agnieszka Woszczyk

Prenoetic Genera in *The Enneads* by Plotinus

ABSTRACT: In the article, I am trying to argue that it is important to distinguish two perspectives in Plotinus's presentation of principal genera. First, from the perspective of an immanent analysis of being, which discloses the understanding of *genus* in the context of the character of noetic world (κόσμος νοητός). This perspective presents ontic categories, i.e. being (τὸ ὄν), motion (κίνησις), rest (στάσις), sameness (ταὐτότης) and difference (ἑτερότης) as internal potent activities of being expressed as the unity of multiplicity. In such a context, the phrase "principles of substance," used to denote the types of being, refers to self--constitution of the Intellect, which occurs as a differentiating internal insight allowing the multiplicity of ideas or minds to emerge. The other perspective involves employing the noetic unity of multiplicity to refer to transcendental principles, i.e. the One and Indefinite Dyad. According to this perspective, γένη τοῦ ὄντος constitute what precedes and facilitates the analysis of being as the unity of multiplicity. Categories which characterize noetic reality, excluding being, now become the very condition of understanding the pre-noetic. Motion, difference, sameness and rest determine the possibility of presenting the dynamics of power of the One, as well as the relation between the One and other (Indefinite Dyad), which is indispensable for constituting the first determined unity of multiplicity. In this context, the expression "principles of substance" gains a meaning of necessary conditions constituting existence and the unity of multiplicity. This expression explains what are the principles of being itself. Such a perspective can be defined as a genetic one, provided that it would not indicate any temporal process of begetting but only finding the conditions which are *sine qua non* for being.

Plotinus's considerations on the genera of being are quite systematically presented in *Enn.* VI. 1 [42], *Enn.* VI. 2 [43] and *Enn.* VI. 3 [44], nevertheless, this question introduced in the *Enneads* is not limited to *Περὶ τῶν γενῶν τοῦ ὄντος* as it could be deduced from the used names of principal genera during explication of such an important issue as transition from the One to many. This is due to the relation between the One and many that the concept of genera of being is a key one from the point of view of Plotinus's metaphysics, quite independently from issues related to the attitude of the author of the *Enneads* to the peripatetic concept of categories, or the stoic theories which he addresses and modifies critically[1]. The reinterpretation of the idea of μέγιστα γένη[2] from Plato's *Sophist* employing an emanational presentation of the activity of the One as the efficient cause[3] is of special importance. It would be crucial to consider the ques-

[1] See G.E. Karamanolis, *Plato and Aristotle in Agreement? Platonists on Aristotle from Antiochus to Porphyry*, Oxford 2006; L.P. Gerson, *The Harmony of Aristotle and Plato According to Neoplatonism*, [in:] *Reading Plato in Antiquity*, eds. H. Tarrant, D. Baltzly, London 2006, pp. 195–221; R. Sorabji, *The Transformation of Plato and Aristotle*, [in:] *Reading Plato…*, *op. cit*, pp. 185–193; R. Sorabji, *The Ancient Commentators on Aristotle*, [in:] *Aristotle Transformed. The Ancient Commentators and Their Influence*, ed. R. Sorabji, London 1990, pp. 1–30; I. Hadot, *The Role of Commentaries on Aristotle in the Teaching of Philosophy According to the Prefaces of the Neoplatonic Commentaries on the 'Categories'*, [in:] *Oxford Studies in Ancient Philosophy*, ed. J. Annas, Supplementary volume, *Aristotle and the Later Tradition*, eds. H. Blumenthal, H. Robinson, Oxford 1991, pp. 175–189; P. Hadot, *The Harmony of Plotinus and Aristotle According to Porphyry*, [in:] *Aristotle Trnasformed…*, *op. cit.*, pp. 125–140; A. Zhyrkova, *The Doctrine of Categories in Neoplatonism*, [in:] *Being or Good? Metamorphoses of Neoplatonizm*, ed. A. Kijewska, Lublin 2004, pp. 85–93; F.J. de Haas, *Did Plotinus and Porphyry Disagree on Aristotle's* Categories*?*, "Phronesis" 2001, vol. 4, pp. 492–526; Ch. Evangeliou, *The Ontological Basis of Plotinus' Criticism of Aristotle's Theory of Categories*, [in:] *The Structure of Being. A Neoplatonic Approach. Studies in Neoplatonism: Ancient and Modern*, vol. IV, ed. R.B. Harris, Norfolk 1982, pp. 78–79.

[2] Christos Evangeliou stresses that Plotinus was the first to introduce an expression *genera of being* (γένη τοῦ ὄντος) into a philosophical dictionary, however Plato uses the term μέγιστα γένη, which means the most general ideas which have the status of ὄντως ὄντα. See Ch. Evangeliou, *op. cit.*, p. 76.

[3] Lloyd P. Gerson defines Plotinian reinterpretation of *megista gene* (*Plotinus*, London – New York 1994, p. 97) as unjustified, and John P. Anton (*Plotinus' Approach to Categorical Theory*, [in:] *The Significance of Neoplatonism, Studies in Neoplatonism: Ancient*

tion whether principal genera can have the status of trans-ontic, or pre-noetic categories. This question can be justified by descriptions of gradual genesis of hypostasis of the Intellect (νοῦς) present in the *Enneads,* in which the transition from the One to noetic reality is presented with the use of principle genera. However, it is worth mentioning at the same time that there is a doubt whether terminological similarity does not result only from metaphorical character of a cataphatic language which Plotinus uses sometimes to explain the unknowable. In my article, I am going to elucidate how specific, generative understanding of a genus which is used by Plotinus, makes from πρῶτα γένη a heuristic tool which enables to conceive the constitution of hypostasis of the Intellect. Consequently, I advocate for reading the parts on "becoming" of the Intellect as an attempt at notional elaboration of "origins of substance," and introducing a pre-noetic dimension, and not only as a metaphorical narration on begetting of existents using a language convention typical for ancient theogonies and gnostic concepts.[4]

It should be mentioned that the expression "pre-noetic dimension of being" seems intrinsically contradictory if we consider that in Plotinus's system, due to equaling being itself with reality of the second hypostasis (νοῦς),[5] this phrase can be synonymously expressed as "pre-ontical dimension of being," which even more strongly emphasizes its contradictory character. Plotinus distinguishes being from becoming, which introduces a typical division for *Enneads* into the realm of a real, eternal, unchangeable being, i.e. *kosmos noetos* (κόσμος νοητός), and the realm of a genetic being which is becoming but never is, i.e. *kosmos aisthetos* (κόσμος αἰσθητός). Simultaneously, he uses the term being to refer to all unity of multiplicity, which he distinguished from the principles of being, the One (ἕν) and Indefinite Dyad (ἀόριστος δύας), and he indicates a fun-

---

and Modern, vol. I, ed. R.B. Harris, Norfolk 1976, pp. 88–89) claims that kinds have a definitely new function in Plotinus, which exceeds far beyond what was suggested by Plato in his dialogue.

[4] See J. Pépin, *Theories of Procession in Plotinus and the Gnostics*, [in:] *Neoplatonism and Gnosticism*, ed. R.T. Wallis, Albany 1992, pp. 297–335.

[5] See *Enn.* III. 6 [26]. 6. 1–33. (Further quotes from Plotinus, *The Enneads*, trans. A.H. Armstrong, vol. I –VII, London 1988).

damental character of being as a definite form of unity.[6] However, these classifications, which are basically in agreement with Platonic tradition, were interpreted in a specific way by Plotinus, since he introduced a triadic structure of hypostases, i.e. the One (ἕν), Intellect (νοῦς) and Soul (ψυχή). Within the structure, Plotinus asks not only what is an ultimate basis of being, and what explains the complexity of its hypostasis, but also he pays a lot of attention to the process of transition from the order of principles to more and more weak forms of ontic unity. In this process, the very problem of emanation of being, thus a question of gradual genesis of noetic reality, acquires a fundamental character. In this context, a question of the pre-noetic occurs because Plotinus distinguishes something different from the principles themselves, but simultaneously something more primordial than the second hypostasis.

Noetic genera

In *Enn.* VI. 2 [43]. 2. 10–14. Plotinus attributes to *genus* generative meaning of being the "principles of substance" (τῆς οὐσίας ἀρχάς). Plotinus explains that these "principles of substance," or genera are what constitutes the nature of existence, what determines it, and what is simultaneously synonymic to it. All that is encompassed by the notion of *being* in the proper sense, which means noetic one, is of a categorical character. Being (τὸ ὄν) as the unity of multiplicity, i.e. the Intellect, cannot be thought without motion (κίνησις) since, as Plotinus writes in *Enn.* VI. 2 [43]. 8. 11–12:

> In its thinking (νοεῖν), then, there is activity (ἐνέργεια) and motion (κίνησις), and in its thinking itself, substance and being.[7]

To which, he adds rest (στάσις) understood as a limit (πέρας) of the Intellect, then difference (ἑτερότης) resulting from the separation of a thinking subject and thought content, and sameness (ταὐτότης) related to the fact

[6] See *Enn.* IV. 1 [4]. 2. 52–55.

[7] Plotinus, *op. cit.*, vol. VI, pp. 134–135.

that everything is contained in the Intellect, due to which noetic multiplicity possesses unity.[8]

> [...] motion, rest, sameness, and otherness – as it is defined by Frans A.J. de Haas – coexist with substance as its constitutive actualities (ἐνέργειαι).[9]

Genus or *kind* means something that essentially possesses generative power, which is the activity of substance, thus it does not predicate a being.[10] Permanence and sameness, and simultaneously dynamics, which are related to motion and difference result from the fact that the Intellect is a subject-object structure. It is the unity of what thinks and what is thought, thus in a more basic dimension, it is the unity of multiplicity which, when considered relationally, emanates from itself unlimited multiplicity.[11] Whereas, everything which emanates within internal structure of the Intellect as a noetic world, is a being since it does not lose sameness and permanence. Consequently, motion and rest, sameness and difference simultaneously and congruously belong to the essence of being. The lack of opposition results from the fact that on the one hand, each kind characterizes different aspect of being, on the other hand, they are not features distinguishing a being, but the very essence of being, or the Intellect.

Kinds enable to explain self-differentiation into multiplicity of minds-ideas characteristic for the Intellect, and retaining of the inner unity simultaneously.[12] Only in (*sc.* noetic) being, sameness and difference, as well as motion and rest can coexist simultaneously. It is stated *explicite* by Plotinu in *Enn.* VI. 2 [43]. 8, when after enumerating genera in the proper sense, i.e. being (τὸ ὄν), motion (κίνησις), rest (στάσις), sameness

[8] See *Enn.* VI. 2 [43]. 8. 18–43.

[9] F.A.J. de Haas, *op. cit.*, p. 514. Anthony C. Lloyd presents their nature in a similar way (*The Anatomy of Neoplatonism*, Oxford 1991, p. 87), and writes that the kinds are not attributes of substance or existence, but their activities.

[10] See *Enn.* VI. 2 [43]. 15. 2–16.

[11] Thus, Plotinus develops Platonic analysis of the one as emanating from itself multiplicity from *Parmenides* 142d–144e, and *passus* from *Timaios* 39e, see, *Enn.* VI. 2 [43]. 22. 1–3 and 13–14.

[12] See *Enn.* VI. 2 [43]. 21. 1–28.

(ταὐτότης) and difference (ἑτερότης), he characterizes their mutual relations as follows:

> These are the primary kinds (πρῶτα δὲ γένη) because you cannot apply any predicate to theme which forms part of the definition of their essence (μηδὲν αὐτῶν κατηγορήσεις ἐν τῷ τί ἐστι). You will certainly predicate being of them (ὄν κατηγορήσεις), for they exist, but nor as their genus (οὐχ ὡς γένος), for they are not particular beings (οὐ γὰρ ὅπερ ὄν τι). [...]. Nor again being participate in these others as if they were its genera: for they do not transcend being are not prior to it (οὐδὲ πρότερα τοῦ ὄντος).[13]

The presentation of the prevalence of one genus over being demonstrates that Plotinus does not wish to treat being as a superior notion, which could undergo division into genera, or reversibly, *being* cannot be derived from genera based on predication[14]. The need to find the first genera does not originate, as it could be assumed, from a wish to classify being into categories, or indicating principal divisions of being in the sense of logical division generating subdivisions of *being*, on the contrary, it originates from the wish to introduce the meaning of existence in the strict sense. It is an attempt to penetrate intellectually intrinsic dynamics which characterize the noetic unity of multiplicity,[15] whose other variants are, among other things, the characteristics of the Intellect regarding the unity of being and truth in presented *Enn.* V. 5 [38]. 1–2, as well as the question of substantial sameness of minds-ideas and the Intellect discussed in *Enn.* V. 9 [5]. 3–9.[16]

However, generative nature of kinds, which explains the possibility of intrinsic self-creation of the Intellect, and existence called the cause of one's own being,[17] constitutes only a partial vision of noetic reality present-

---

[13] *Enn.* VI. 2 [43]. 8. 43–50; p. 137.

[14] Indirectly, it is indicated by argumentation in *Enn.* VI. 2 [43]. 19–20, in these chapters Plotinus considers an issue similar to the question of existence prevailing over genera, i.e. prevalence of the Intelligence over its content-ideas.

[15] See *Enn.* VI. 2 [43]. 22. 7–21.

[16] See *Enn.* VI. 2 [43]. 4. 13–19.

[17] See *Enn.* VI. 7 [38]. 2. 23–27.

ed in the *Enneads*. Following the title question of *Enn.* VI. 7 [38], i.e. *How the multitude of the forms came into being, and on the Good?,* it is worth investigating whether calling genera *principles of substance* (τῆς οὐσίας ἀρχάς) in *Enn.* VI. 2 [43]. 2. 10–14 has any additional meaning if we do not analyze being within immanent characteristics as it has been done so far, by studying the structure of the noetic unity of multiplicity, but in the relation to the One.

Transcendental determination of being

An internal relation within the Intellect, i.e. the relation between the Intellect and ideas-minds, indicates that being must contain the source of its own differentiation or division into the multiplicity of ideas--minds. While, this explanation may amount to proving a generic structure of being, the explication of conditions of existence as the unity of multiplicity must refer to the transcendental principles, namely the One (ἕν) and Indefinite Dyad (ἀόριστος δύας).[18] However, the possibility of distinguishing between the unity of multiplicity and the One as a principle indicates that conceiving their relation can occur without referring to the category of difference between the One and other than the One, or unlimited multiplicity. Correspondingly, Plotinus's use of emanation metaphors in his descriptions of constituting of the second hypostasis is based on a motif of movement from the One toward the multiplicity. This indicates the need to characterize a pre-noetic dimension by employing terminology which takes into consideration γένη τοῦ ὄντος.

In *Enn.* II. 4 [12]. 5. 28–37, Plotinus presents the question of the genesis of the Intellect as follows:

> For Otherness there exists always (ἡ ἑτερότης ἡ ἐκεῖ ἀεί), which produces intelligible matter (ἡ τὴν ὕλην ποιεῖ);

[18] I will not justify here the duality of principles in the Plotinian system, since I would have go beyond the scope of my paper to present this issue properly. See A. Woszczyk, *Problem "hen" i "aoristos dyas" w "Enneadach" Plotyna*, Katowice 2007.

> for this is the principle (ἀρχή) of matter, this and the primary Movement. For his reason Movement, too, was called Otherness, because Movement and Otherness sprang forth together. The Movement and Otherness which came from the First are undefined (ἀόριστον δὲ καὶ ἡ κίνησις καὶ ἡ ετερότης), and need the First to define them; and they are defined when they turn to it (ὁρίζεται δέ, ὅταν πρὸς αὐτὸ ἐπιστραφῇ). But before the turning, matter too, was undefined and the Other (ἀόριστον καί ἡ ὕλη καὶ τὸ ἕτερον) and not yet good, but unilluminated from the First (ἀφώτιστον). For if light comes from the First, then that which receives the light, before it receives it has everlastingly no light; but it has light as other than itself, since the light comes to it from something else.[19]

These comments refer to noetic matter (ἡ νοητὴ ὕλη) which is eternal but whose genesis can be presented, or to be more precise, the genesis of the Intellect, since, according to Plotinus, eternal entities also can be considered as begotten because they have an origin.[20] Thus, it is possible to differentiate certain purely abstract stages of constituting the Intellect, where the first one is based on endless movement and difference, and a subsequent stage is a turn (ἐπιστροφή) toward the One in which a primordial otherness defined itself forming νοῦς[21] the pre-noetic status of difference is unquestionable here, and reveals also an important *novum*,

---

[19] Plotinus, *op. cit.*, vol. II, p. 117.

[20] See *ibidem*, p. 190, *Enn.* II. 4 [12]. 5. 25–28. This principle is further elucidated by Porphyry (*Sententiae* 14. 1–13), See *Porphyre Sentences*, ed. L. Brisson, T. 1–2, Paris 2005.

[21] See *Enn.* V. 2 [11]. 1. 8–16. Usually, the constitution of the Intellect is most generally presented as a result of a three-phase process which includes emerging of an indefinite emanated being from the One, which is most frequently identified as the Indefinite Dyad or noetic matter, which then turns to its origin, and this act is equal to self-identification and being fully actualized by the Intellect, understood as a self--thinking thought. Independently of resolving certain detailed issues, this model is accepted by R. Arnou, *Le désir d Dieu dans la philosophie de Plotyn*, Paris 1921, p. 196; É. Bréhier, *The Philosophy of Plotinus*, trans. by J. Thomas, Chicago 1958, p. 136; J.M. Rist, *The Indefinite Dyad and Intelligible Matter in Plotinus*, "Classical Quarterly" 1962, vol. 12, pp. 99–107; A.H. Armstrong, *The Architecture of the Intelligible Universe in the Philosophy of Plotinus*, Amsterdam 1967; A.C. Lloyd, *op. cit.*, pp. 155–186; J. Bussanich, *The One and Its Relation to Intellect in Plotinus. A Commentary on the Selected Texts*, Leiden, New York, København, Köln 1998.

which is introduced by Neo-Platonism to a reflection on the One-being relation constituted by the Platonic tradition. This novelty involves the presentation of reality employing the categories of power (δύναμις) and activity (ἐνέργεια),[22] however, the activity is no longer connected with substance, and it does not imply being as a carrier conditioning only the possibility of activity. In W *Enn.* VI. 8 [39] 20. 9–16, Plotinus states this directly when he describes the activity of the One:

> Nor should we be afraid to assume that the first activity (ἐνέργειαν τὴν πρώτην) is without substance (ἄνευ οὐσίας), but posit this very fact as his, so to speak, existence (ὑπόστασιν). But if one posited an existence without activity, the principle would be defective and the most perfect of all imperfect. And if one adds activity one does not keep the One. If then the activity is more perfect than the substance (τελειότερον ἡ ἐνέργεια τῆς οὐσίας), and the first [*sc*. The One] is most perfect, the first will be activity (πρώτη ἂν ἐνέργεια εἴη).[23]

This passage shows that Plotinus recognizes the primacy of activity over substance, and negating a peripatetic principle of the priority of substance is necessary to explain a causative activity of the One, which is being beyond being.[24] It is impossible to declare that the One "is" since it will eliminate the absolute oneness.[25] Clearly, Plotinus is not speaking here only metaphorically, if he were using metaphors, he would admit that it is impossible to think the One differently than as being, for that reason he would introduce predication about the One based on an inadequate language of existence. Meanwhile, he denies the One existence but he still claims that the One acts, what is more, he acknowledges that the activity is more perfect than substance, thus more primal than being. This is indicated by the context of his statement, since the *passus* which proceeds it refers

---

[22] S.E. Gersh, *KINHESIS AKINHTOS. A Study of Spiritual Motion in the Philosophy of Proclus*, Leiden 1973, p. 3.

[23] Plotinus, *op. cit.*, vol. VII, pp. 292–293.

[24] This principle is also questioned while evil is being considered in order to show that matter acts by weakening oneness which is attributed to beings, although it is not a being, see *Enn.* I. 8 [51]. 6. 28–34.

[25] See *Enn.* VI. 9 [9]. 5. 25–39.

to the difference between the One as the causative activity itself, which is not directed to any specific object,[26] unlike the Intellect twofold in its activity into subject and object.[27] The context does not allow us to accept an interpretation which would indicate the limitations of a cataphatic language while referring to the One, and would also accept its activity only in a metaphorical sense. Leaving aside the question of cognitive possibility of presenting the One, since it is another issue, we can say that Plotinus aims at presenting the One as causative power which acts despite the fact that this activity is of beyond substantial nature.

This flow of power, which is the image of the activity of everything that can be a principle, is the basis for notional distinction between actualized and non-actualized stages during the constitution of hypostases, thus it facilitates avoiding paradoxes inscribed in thinking about being beyond being. Since existence is considered as actualization, i.e. as turning back toward a principle, it is only being in the proper sense. Consequently, a pre-epistophic stage is something that can be examined using categories of being different from an efficient cause but, simultaneously, examined as a pre-existential stage, unformed in the movement back to its limiting cause. Therefore, an efficient cause reveals motion and difference, to which an efficient cause gives definiteness and sameness. If the One is active and manifests itself as the uniting power, therefore according to the metaphor of emanation, what is the One itself can be distinguished from operating power of the One.[28]

In other words, though the existentially transcendent One is beyond conceivability, simultaneously it can be negatively conceived as *other* than what appears as its oneness from the immanent perspective of being. This difference is based on the concept of twofold activity, i.e. the internal and external activity of substance, which is presented by Plotinus in *Enn.* V. 4 [7]. 2. 27–39:

---

[26] Plotinus characterizes the One in opposition to noetic being, e.g. in *Enn.* VI. 9 [9]. 6. 42–44, claiming that the One does not possess any difference, or movement because it does not think.

[27] See *Enn.* VI. 8 [39]. 19. 12–20.

[28] See *Enn.* VI. 6 [32]. 13. 55–69.

> [...] there is an activity which belongs to substance and one which goes out from substance (ἡ μέν ἐστι τῆς οὐσίας, ἡ δ' ἐκ τῆς οὐσίας ἑκάστον); and that which belongs to substance is the active actuality which is each particular thing, and the other activity derives from that first one, and must in everything be a consequence of it, different from the thing itself: as in the fire there is a heat which is content of its substance, and another which comes into being from that primary heat [...]. So it is also in the higher world [...].[29]

Importantly, when Plotinus emphasizes otherness of both activities, he indicates also that it is necessary to include a differentiating factor. The acting One, and the activity of hypostasis occurs inevitably, is the one which diversifies into the One and the activity of the One.

Going back to the above-quoted passage from *Enn.* II. 4 [12]. 5. 28–37, it can be added that eternal difference and motion occur as pre-noetic kinds inscribed into an emanative causality of the One, but not only as noetic kinds. This causes a certain difficulty, since the activities of the One can be categorized only by dualistic notions independently from the attitude toward the origin or independence of *aoristos dyas* from the One. Plotinus writes about the origin of the Intellect in *Enn.* VI. 7 [38]. 8. 18–27:

> Now it is clear that his one must be many, because it exists after the altogether One [...]. But what prevents it from being a dyad (δυάδα)? Now each of the ones in the dyad could not be absolutely one, but must again be at least two, and again it is the same with each of those; and then there was in the first dyad (ἐν τῇ δυάδι τῇ πρώτῃ) movement (κίνησις) all well as rest (στάσις), and there was also intellect (νοῦς) [...].[30]

This passage indicates that the distinction between the One and not one is discussed by Plotinus with reference to principles as a difference between the One and Indefinite Dyad.[31] Not one appears as multiplicity due to limitless self-multiplicability of a dyad. Indirectly, it is also suggested that the first dyad can be identified with difference, since like difference from *Enn.*

---

[29] Plotinus, *op. cit.*, vol. V, pp. 146–149.

[30] *Ibidem*, vol. VII, pp. 110–111.

[31] Especially when compared to *Enn.* V. 4 [7]. 2. 5–13.

II. 4 [12]. 5. 28–37 it is a condition preceding constituting of the Intellect. While inside the definite Intellect, at the stage actualized by being directed to the highest value represented by the One, we can speak of a definite dyad instead of *aoristos dyas.*[32] This justifies again the fact that difference cannot only refer to a noetic dimension, namely to the sphere of being in the proper sense, but it must precede being as an unlimited multiplicity determined by the One. In *Enn.* VI. 2 [43], Plotinus warns against giving being or any other genus a primary position in relation to the others. Meanwhile, in light of this indicated relation between the One, at least difference and movement appear as πρότερα and ἐπαναβέβεκα in relation to being. Taking into account the quoted passages, it can be assumed that movement and difference are characterized as indefinite or limitless. This suggests their non-being character, due to the fact that being must be of a definite form, and the higher its oneness (definiteness) the more perfect being it is. Indefinite motion and difference are what emanates from the One, but does not yet have a status of being. Descriptions of the conditions of being formation using language of a pre-noetic process, hence revealing "emergence" of reality of the second hypostasis (νοῦς), suggest that emanating of being from non--being (being beyond being) assumes motion and difference, but not only these two kinds. In *Enn.* V. 2 [11]. 1. 8–16, rest (στάσις) is also presented as something preceding being:

> [...] the One, perfect, because it seeks nothing, has nothing and needs nothing, overflows (ὑπερερρύη) as it were, and its superbundance (ὑπερπλῆρες) makes something other than itself (πεποίηκεν ἄλλο). This, when it has come into being, turns back upon the One and is filled, and becomes Intellect by looking towards it. Its halt (στάσις) and turning towards the One constitutes being, its gaze upon the One, Intellect.[33]

It does not seem accidental that when Plotinus defined rest in relation to a noetic sphere, he linked it to an idea as a limit (πέρας) of the Intellect. In the quoted passage, rest is related to the One, in which yet an indefinite emanated being turns itself toward the One, which has a determining and

[32] See *Enn.* V. 1 [32]. 5. 6–22.
[33] Plotinus, *op. cit.*, vol. V, pp. 58–59.

limiting function. However, adding another kind means that explaining being in relations to the One consequently requires accepting sameness (ταὐτότης), analogically to the sameness of being. The latter was singled out by Plotinus because of oneness of the Intellect, whereas in a pre-noetic dimension it should be associated analogically with the One as a condition of oneness of being. The nature of difference (ἑτερότης), which as a kind of being was determined based on distinction between a thinking subject and what is thought, in the pre-noetic dimension was presented as distinctiveness from the One. Whereas motion (κίνησις), defined as the activity of the Intellect, in a pre-noetic dimension is used to define the transition from the One to many, as well as the return to the One.

Nonetheless, it should be clearly explained that neither motion nor difference, which occur as characteristics of a non-substantial activity of the One, neither rest nor sameness, necessary for the explanation of targeting an indefinite emanated being at the One, do not translate into cognitive perspective of the nature of principles of being using ontological categories. This possibility can be questioned due to at least two reasons. Firstly, what I call here *pre-noetic genera* is not the same as noetic genera. This is because noetic genera were characterized by unity guaranteed by definiteness of being, while motion and difference in pre-being or pre-ontic dimension must be presented as indefinite, since only as these which do not refer to the One can appear as distinct from being and its generic characteristics. Yet, as indefinite they are unknowable, since what does not have a limit or measure cannot be cognized. Secondly, in pre-noetic relation of the One and Indefinite Dyad, generic concepts are of an aproximative nature. It becomes especially evident for sameness and rest, which do not allow a real presentation of the nature of the One as a condition of "actualization" of the Intellect. They are cognitive approximations, and facilitate distinguishing in the relation of the One and other, the element due to which *other* can transform from indefiniteness to an organized noetic multiplicity, without stating anything about the One and Indefinite Dyad themselves. Since the noetic relation between one-many, which characterizes being, is derived from the relation between the One and Indefinite Dyad, πρῶτα γένη reveal their heuristic usefulness as metaphysical concepts by forming the only possible language to grasp what exceeds the structure of being, simultaneously constituting the condition of understanding them.

To sum up, in Plotinus's presentation of the principal kinds, it is important to distinguish two perspectives:

- an immanent analysis of being, which reveals the understanding of a *kind* within the context of the nature of noetic world (κόσμος νοητός). This perspective shows ontic kinds, i.e. being (τὸ ὄν), motion (κίνησις), rest (στάσις), sameness (ταὐτότης) and difference (ἑτερότης) as internal powers of the being activity, being understood as the unity of multiplicity. In such a context, an expression "principles of substance", employed to denote kinds of being, refers to self-constitution of the Intellect, which occurs as a differentiating internal insight determining the multiplicity of ideas-minds;
- a relation of noetic one-many to transcendental principles, namely the One and Indefinite Dyad. From such a perspective, γένη τοῦ ὄντος are what precedes and facilitates the analysis of being as the unity of multiplicity. The kinds which characterize noetic reality, excluding being, occur now as a condition of understanding the pre-noetic. Thanks to motion, difference, sameness and rest it is possible to present the dynamics of power of the One, and the relation between the One and other (Indefinite Dyad) which is necessary to form the first definite unity of multiplicity. In this context, an expression "principles of substance" acquires the meaning of necessary conditions constituting being as the unity of multiplicity, explaining the basis of being. This perspective can be called generic, provided that it does not indicate any temporal process of begetting, but only finding necessary conditions of being.

Jacek Surzyn

Disjunctives as Transcategorial Attributes of Being – An Outline of John Duns Scotus's Standpoint

ABSTRACT: The article is an attempt to outline John Duns Scotus's stance in the discussion on disjunction as one of the aspects of understanding transcategorial attributes of being. Scotus's understanding of disjunction contributed to a different look at Aristotelian categories, which, undoubtedly, opened up the route towards their re-interpretation in modern times. Kant's approach to categories inferred from judgments corresponds largely to Scotus's conception of disjunctives. Kant saw categories as pairs of interconnected attributes exhausting the subjective content, which was the foundation of Scotus's thought. In Scotus's conception, disjunctives are attributes transcending the categorial structure and attributed only to being as such (*ens inquantum ens*). Taken separately, the disjunctive attributes only partially exhaust the notion of being; together as a disjunctive pair, they are coextensive with being. On this view, each disjunctive pair is convertible with being as such (being qua being).

John Duns Scotus is the author of an original conception of disjunctives as transcategorial attributes of being. Scotus's understanding of disjunction contributed to a different look at Aristotelian categories and opened up the route towards a new approach to categories in modern times. Not incidentally, Kant's conceiving of categories (inferred from judgments) concurs largely with Scotus's proposition of disjunctives. Kant conceived of categories as pairs of interconnected attributes that exhaust the subjective content, which seemed to be the essence of Scotus's idea. In Scotus's conception, disjunctives are the attributes transcending the categorial structure and thereby attributed only to *being qua being* (*ens inquantum ens*). Taken separately, each disjunctive attribute always only partially exhausts (delimits) the notion of being. Nonetheless, taken together as a pair, they are coextensive with being, and thereby remain exchangeable with being; on this view, each pair of disjunctives is convertible with being. In Scotus's thought, the disjunctive attributes as trans-categories perform a significant role in the construction of science (knowledge) of God. With reference to God, Scotus does not employ simple transcendentals convertible with *being qua being* but the disjunctives. Scotus's list of disjunctive attributes is long yet in none of his works did he propose a complete list. However, it is possible to identify the most important disjunctive pairs; they include necessary-contingent, infinite-finite, dependent-independent, absolute-relative, prior-posterior, non-composite-composite, unity-plurality, cause-effect, substance-accident, act-potency, exceeding-exceeded, finite-indeterminate, similar-different and equal-unequal.[1]

---

[1] See: E. Gilson, *Jean Duns Scot. Introduction à ses positions fondamentales*, Paris 1952, p. 129, 210, 271, pp. 186–189, 315–317; E.I. Zieliński, *Nieskończoność bytu Bożego w filozofii Jana Dunsa Szkota*, Lublin 1980, pp. 32–33. Regarding the convertibility of disjunction, Wolter writes the following: "This disjunction, like countless others, is equivalent to a simple convertible transcendental attribute of being: Istud disjunctum necessarium vel possibile, est passio entis circum loquens illimitata in entibus", A.B. Wolter, *The Transcendentals and Their Function in the Metaphysics of Duns Scotus*, New York 1946, p. 128, footnote 1. Further on in the same footnote Wolter quotes the commentary of the Scotist Franciscus Lychetus on the above (it is included in Vivés' edition of *Opera Omnia*, X, 626 b): "Passiones disiunctae circumloquuntur aliquam passionem convertibilem cum ente, ut necessarium vel possibile, non tamen sic intelligendo quod totum disjunctum possit esse unum imcomplexum, nec unum totum incomplexum includens,

Each pair of disjunctives is convertible with being but not to the same extent as they may be either naturally or formally opposite; that is to say, the attributes may be naturally opposed like actual-potential, or formally opposed like independent-dependent. Nevertheless, all the disjunctions of properties are similar in that in every one of them, one member is a simple negation of the other and so they are absolute opposites of each other. Moreover, a number of disjunctions do not presuppose (*a priori*) that being must be either of the opposites. For instance, prior-posterior implies a plurality of things while the disjunction exceeding-exceeded presupposes the existence of several beings related to one another in gradable order, that is to say, being equal by essence. In the first group of disjunctions which do not a priori assume anything but rather induce certain state, in addition to the disjunction prior-posterior, Scotus also includes the disjunction cause-effect. The difference is determined by the internal content of individual members of disjunction. If disjunction occurs between two contradictory opposites, there is no need to establish its convertible character. Being is either one or the other with no alternative and so the disjunction itself completely exhausts being; the disjunction is perfect in the sense of correlation which does not in any way pertain to the actual content of being. In the case of the disjunctives mentioned before, it is necessary to seek for a proof of their convertible character as this cannot be inferred from purely logical principles but recourse must be made to experience.[2] With correlatives, the existence of one notion – following

immo necessario plura incomplexa includit, sed dicitur circumloqui, quia habetur loco unius incomplexio […], passio vero disiuncta tantum convertitur ratione totius disjuncti, et non ratione alicuius partis tantum, ut portet quia haec est vera: omne ens est necessarium vel possibile, et haec falsa: omne ens est necessarium, et similitur ista: omne ens est passionem disjunctam, quia passio incomplexa convertitur cum ente, ut est indifferens ad omnia inferiora, non dolendo signum distributirum, ut ens est unum, verum, bonum, tamen haec non est vera absolute ens ut ens est necessarium vel possibile, abstrahit enim ab utraque, Licet enim omne ens sit necessarium vel possibile, non tamen ens ut ens, sicut etiam haec est vera: omne animal est rationale vel irrationale, non tamen haec est vera: animal ut animal est rationale vel irrationale". Lychetos seems to have perfectly rendered Scotus's intuition about the convertibility of disjunctions different from the convertibility of simple attributes of being.

2 See A.B. Wolter, *op. cit.*, p. 129. In this sense, regarding the pair prior-posterior Scotus writes the following: "Est ergo aliquod ens prius non posterius, et aliquod posterius et

the principle of full correlation – implies the other – since one cannot speak of being as posterior and vice versa.[3]

Such a fine and intricate distinction is extremely important in Scotus's thought. On that basis, it becomes possible to prove the existence of God from the premise that there exists necessary relationship, for instance, between caused and cause. Something is caused only when it is produced by cause; thus through empirical experience of the caused effect, one may infer the existence of its cause on the grounds of logical necessity. So understood, disjunctions, as A.B. Wolter puts it "form the framework of metaphysics as natural theology", which can only be achieved if the transcendental structure of the disjunctive attributes of being is established since the point of departure here is their correlative relation to being as such. In other words, it is necessary to establish a full determination of such being which in itself has absolute simplicity and lacks all determination that does not exclude its becoming this or that.[4] Hence an essential role is attributed by Scotus to disjunctive transcendentals regarding the knowledge of God: that He is and who He is.

The objectives of metaphysics in this respect consist then in devising a synthetic transcendental structure and exploring logical dependences between its constituent elements; that is to say, an internal coherence facili-

non prius, nullum autem quin vel prius vel posterius". See English translation: John Duns Scotus, *A Treatise on God as First Principle*, trans. by A.B. Wolter, Chicago 1966, p. 48. What would the difference consist in here? To put it simply, as regards being, the disjunctions prior-posterior, cause-effect exhaust it fully and completely as, in addition to the alternative either-or, they entail that if something is prior, then there must be something posterior, and if something is a cause, then something must be caused. Thus the alternative turns into conjunction. With reference to other disjunctions the situation is different, for instance necessity-contingency does not entail that there exist both necessary being and contingent being but in terms of logic it entails only that either this or that.

[3] See: *Quaestiones super libros Metaphysicorum Aristotelis* (onwards quoted as QSMet.) I, q. 1, n. 47 (I, 27–28). I quote Scotus's works according to the edition: Ioannes Duns Scoti *Opera Omnia* (editio minor). A cura di Giovanni Lauriola. Editrice Alberobello 1998–2001, vol. I–III. I identify this edition by the following: Latin numeral – number of the volume, Arabic numeral – number of the part of the volume, number after the coma – page number.

[4] Comp. A.B. Wolter, *op. cit.*, p. 130.

tating the attainment of Primus. Duns Scotus derived his ideas from Avicenna, unlike most of his contemporaries, who accepted natural (physical) basis of knowledge of God – *scientia divina* – with a subordinate status of metaphysics (advocated by Averroes, but also by Thomas Aquinas). The supreme knowledge available to a human being was the knowledge of God based on a very concrete point of departure marked by common sensorial cognition and the process of abstraction.[5] This fitted within the Averroes's interpretation of Aristotle in which, generally speaking, the point was that God's existence could be proven through his being the first cause of motion – the Prime mover. Scotus points to the ostensibility of this assumption: even if God is the acknowledged *Primum Movens*, this "primacy" is assumed from metaphysical rather than physical premises. Scotus thus enters into a dispute between Avicenna and Averroes favouring Avicenna's conception.[6] He himself tries to establish proof in support of God's existence differently, by rejecting the traditional Aristotelian principle: "whatever is moved, it is moved by something else".[7]

Starting with the same premise Scotus argues with the Augustinian tradition represented by Alexander of Hales and Saint Bonaventure whose arguments for the existence of God were based on the notions of truth and good.[8] Scotus was quite convinced that Avicenna seeking the autonomy of metaphysics demonstrated better intuition in this regard. Metaphysics, as Scotus holds, facilitates constructing a credible proof of the existence of God based on the disjunctive transcendentals analyzed

---

[5] It is done by Thomas Aquinas; therefore, in his conception there occurs the obviousness of being and analogy of being, while in Scotus's thought, there is the equivalence of being.

[6] "Dico quod Avicenna cui contadixit »bene dixit« et Commentator male", *Ordinatio* (onwards quoted as Ord.) prol., p. 3, q. 3, n. 21 (III/1, 49). Comp. QSMet. VI, q. 4, n. 3 (I, 305).

[7] Scotus criticises this principle in: Ord. II, d. 3, q. 7, n. 27 (III/1, 937–938); Ord. II, d. 25, q. unica, n. 12–13 (III/1, 1169–1170). Detailed overview of Scotus's standpoint, see: E. Bettoni, *L'Ascesa a Dio in Duns Scoto*, Milan 1943, pp. 7–18.

[8] A.B. Wolter, *op. cit.*, pp. 131–132. As regards the Augustinian tradition, see: A. Daniels, *Quellenbeiträge und Untersuchungen zur Geschichte der Gottesbeweise in dreizehnten Jahrhundert mit bessonderer Berücksichtingung des Arguments im Proslogion des bl. Anselm,* Münster 1909.

within its framework. Here a point of departure is the logical law of full disjunction on the basis of which one can find absolute determinations of being in metaphorical dimension (following Avicenna) as *ens inquantum ens*, that is to say, as that which is primarily deduced by intellect. Interestingly, Scotus's disjunction is concurrent with some conclusions of Saint Bonaventure. In fact, Bonaventure did employ disjunction to prove the existence of God on the basis of the ten self-evident assumptions and conclusions.[9] Broadly speaking, they are derived from simple schemas of the implication: *if… …then* and in this sense, they fulfill the fundamental condition of inference posited by Aristotle that any order of scholarly argumentation begins with that which is necessary, obvious and true:

> Assuming then that my thesis as to the nature of scientific knowing is correct, the premisses of demonstrated knowledge must be true, primary, immediate, better known than and prior to the conclusion, which is further related to them as effect to cause. Unless these conditions are satisfied, the basic truths will not be "appropriate" to the conclusion.[10]

In this we can clearly see the basic meaning of the law of disjunction; the disjunction which eventually boils down to the absolute opposites: either A or B most fully expresses the difference among being since the

---

[9] Prima est ista: omne verum omnibus mentibus impressum est verum indubitabile. – Secunda est ista: omne verum, quod omnis creatura proclamat, est verum indubitabile. – Tertia est ista : omne verum in se ipso certissimum et evidentissimum est verum indubitabile", s. Bonaventura, *Quaestiones disputatae de mysterio Ss. Trinitatis*, q. 1, a. 1, [in:] s. Bonaventurae *Opera Omnia* studio et cura Collegii a s. Bonaventura, tomus V, Ad Clara Aquas 1887, p. 45. These ten suppositions are presented on pp. 141–143 (arguments 11–20). The significance of this text was emphasized by A.B. Wolter (*op. cit.*, pp. 132–134) who also noted that these arguments were not fully appreciated by E. Gilson in his work on Saint Bonaventure (E. Gilson, *La philosophie de Saint Bonaventure*, Paris 1924).

[10] Aristotle, *Posterior Analytics* I, chapter 2, trans. by G.R.G. Mure, Adelaide 2007, 71b 19–22. See J. Salamucha, *The Notion of Inference in Aristotle and Saint Thomas Aquinas*, [in:] J. Salamucha, *Knowledge and Faith. Selected Writings in Philosophy*, Lublin 1997, p. 245. Comp. Aristotle's arguments in his *Metaphysics* VII, chapter 15, 1039 b 31–1040 a 2.

opposites divide being completely. A good example might be the second argument of Bonaventure:

> If being exists from something else, then also exists being not from something else, and because nothing carries out itself from nonentity to entity, it follows the principle of carrying out has necessarily to be in first being, which does not be carry out by something else. If the being coming from something else is the same, what created being, and being not carrying out from something else is the same, what uncreated being, which is God, then from every difference of beings results God's existence.[11]

Bonaventure points out that there is a difference between beings which Scotus formulates as a pair of alternative opposites. Thus the disjunctives are primary attributes of being qua being. Scotus calls them *primae differentiae entis* emphasizing the logical condition for the occurrence of those ultimate differences and primary determinants of being. Interestingly, Bonaventure himself resigns from inferring the existence of God from the sensual perception of physical movement that is to say, from that which was moved to the mover. Instead, he takes into account the logical aspect of motion-change; thus a point of departure for him is the ability to be moved while the cause is what causes this ability while not being moved and changeable itself.[12]

Drawing on Bonaventure's conclusions Scotus modifies the latter's standpoint. He changes the logical implication into an unconditioned alternative starting with the premise *if something, then something else*. In the ultimate categories pertaining to the transcendental being he draws an absolute distinction of being: if an implication is true and unconditioned, then we deal with an absolute distinction (determination) – if there exists being that is moved (able to be moved), then there exists being that is moving (able to move) and so eventually, being unconditionally diversifies into the moved and the moving.[13]

---

[11] s. Bonaventura, *op. cit.*, p. 46.

[12] *Ibidem*, p. 47. Comp. A.B. Wolter, *op. cit.*, p. 136.

[13] It is worth noting that Scotus and Bonaventure differ about denominating these conditions as self-evident – *per se notae*. Bonaventure seeks the source in illumination whereas Scotus invokes logical necessity.

We should now present Scotus's definition of the universal logical law of disjunction of the attributes of being, which he formulates as follows:

> In the case of proprieties of disjunction, though only disjunction should not be deduced from being, however beginning as general principle form less perfect extremity of some being has been possible to conclude that different more perfect extremity of some being appears in some different being. Similarly proof: if some being would be finite, then some being should be infinite. If some being is accidental, then some being is necessary. In such kind of cases in reference to larger imperfection of extremity in frames of disjunction has been possible to predicate about individual being only then, when the larger perfection of extremity will be predicated on a being from it depends.[14]

Let us note that Scotus formulates the law of disjunction in a manner that the existence of one of its members does not imply the existence of the other superior member. The other member, as Scotus emphasizes, is deduced through concluding or a longer process of inference, that is to say, the entire process of argumentation. So understood, disjunction has a wide variety of applications in Scotus's thought. In metaphysics, it is used to determine the internal properties of being while in theology, it enables us to gain knowledge of God conceived of as an infinite being.

Before we focus on investigating the operating principle of disjunction, we should make an attempt at classifying all the transcendental disjunctions. As previously indicated, they can be classified as the attributes of being. Scotus however, does not propose a complete list of disjunctives; in fact, he leaves the list open. What he intends to do is to demonstrate the principle of disjunction as an absolute determination of

---

[14] "In passionibus autem disjunctis, licet illud totum disjunctum non possit demonstrari de ente, tamen communitur supposito illa extremo quod est minus nobile de aliquo ente, potest concludi aliud extremum quod est nobilius de aliquo ente, sicut sequitur; si aliquod ens est finitum, ergo aliquod ens est infinitum, et si aliquod ens est contingens, ergo aliquod ens est necessarium; quia in talibus non posset enti particularitor in esse imperfectius extremum, nisi alicui enti in esset perfectius extremum a quo dependeret", Ord. I, d. 38, q. unica, n. 5 (III/1, 715).

being allowing for its transition from pure capacity for existence to beings as individual entities. Scotus then enumerates a number of disjunctive attributes to exemplify the difference between them and the simple absolute properties convertible with being, unity, truth and goodness. He also notices that many more can be indicated.[15]

Let us now take a closer look into the disjunctions proposed by Scotus and let us make an attempt at their classification. The four disjunctions are identical with Saint Bonaventure's assumptions: prior-posterior,[16] independent-dependent,[17] necessary-contingent[18] and absolute-relative.[19] Others are to a great extent similar to Bonaventure's theses. Following the order of Bonaventure's theses we have the premise number 15:

> If diminished being exists, it means being in respect to, then exists also being in every respect to,[20]

which can be compared with Scotistic distinction between a finite and infinite being.[21] The premise number 16:

> If being exists through respect to some anather being, then exists also being per se. [...] Since therefore the totality of remaining beings should be subordinate it, then with totality of things has brought so about existence, as about cognition of God,[22]

---

[15] See: Ord. I, d. 38, q. unica, n. 5 (III/1, 715).

[16] See: John Duns Scotus, *op. cit.*, chapter 4, pp. 47–48. Comp.: "si est ens posterius, est et ens prius, quia posterius non est nisi a priori: si ergo est universitas posteriorum, necesse est, esse ens primus", s. Bonaventura, *op. cit.*, p. 46.

[17] *Ord.* I, d. 8, p. 1, q. 3, 2–3 (III/1, 385–387). Comp.: "Item, si est ens ab alio, est ens non ab alio: quia nihil educit se ipsum de nonesse in esse", s. Bonaventura, *op. cit.*, p. 46. Bonaventure writes about *ens a se* and *ens ab alio.*

[18] *Ord.* I, d. 8, p. 1, q. 3, 2–3 (III/1, 385–387). Comp. in Bonaventure: "Item, si est ens possibile, est ens necessarium: quia possibile dicit indifferentiam ad esse et nonesse", s. Bonaventura, *op. cit.*, p. 46.

[19] Comp. in Bonaventure: "Item, si est ens respectivum, est ens absolutum: quia respectivum nunquam terminatur nisi ad absolutum", s. Bonaventura, *op. cit.*, p. 46.

[20] *Ibidem*, p. 47.

[21] Comp. A.B. Wolter, *op. cit.*, p. 139.

[22] s. Bonaventura, *op. cit.*, p. 47.

in Scotus's thought will correspond to the disjunction end-that which has an end. The first member here is a being in itself as an end (or a goal), while the being acting for an end (being on its way to the goal) is a finalized being, that is a being existing by virtue of something else.[23] As for the premise number 17:

> If being exists by participation, then the being exists from essence, because participation has predicated solely in relation to something, what posseses something else from essence, for all, what is accident moves to some existence per se,[24]

we have the disjunction: cause-effect, because Bonaventure relies here on the notion of participation, whereas in Scotus an assumption primarily refers to finitude or limitation, that is to the disjunction of cause-effect and secondarily to the previously indicated disjunctions of infinite--finite and absolute-relative. Scotus identifies more disjunctions yet they are subordinate to the above mentioned. They include: act-potency and simple-complex which boil down to the distinctions: infinite-finite and absolute-relative,[25] or, they do not pertain directly to God and as such they are secondary disjunctions. The list of the latter includes: one-many, end--that which has an end, substance-accident, similar-different, and equal--unequal. The idea that guides Scotus in establishing the disjunctions is not providing the finite list of disjunctions but rather demonstrating the metaphysical nature of the principle itself. This is first and foremost re-

[23] Scotus will attribute this to the order of dependence: that which is posterior divides itself into four corresponding elements, see: John Duns Scotus, *op. cit.*, chapter 1, p. 8. Regarding the latter, we can distinguish "final" – in the original version *finitum*, in the footnote (*ibidem*, footnote 18, p. 110) explained as follows: "Scotus uses on description of this, what would be directed to aim, term *finitum*, which in this case possesses completely different meaning than in classic Latin – it means: appointed with borders, definited, completed, determined and so on […]. *Finitum* denotes this, what is the result of acting of finited causa".

[24] s. Bonaventura, *op. cit.*, p. 47.

[25] See A.B. Wolter, *op. cit.*, p. 139. The author distinquishes the metaphysical rather than physical status of Scotus's disjunctions: "Scotus make no mention of the disjunction ens mutabile-ens immutabile, since the ens mobile is not property the object of metaphysics but of physics" (*ibidem*, pp. 139–140).

flected in the law of disjunction which constitutes the basic law of full internal determination of being as such. From this point of view, it is crucial that we should make a distinction between disjunctions primarily convertible with being and disjunctions operating by way of alternative exclusion of one of its opposite members. On that basis, it is possible to classify all disjunctions by their essence.

The first group encompasses disjunctions absolutely convertible with being indicated at the beginning of this chapter, including prior-posterior, end-that which has an end and cause-caused. Scotus distinguishes the disjunctions fully convertible with being upon the fundamental premise that we actually deal with the universal order of all things: whatever may exist, is ordered. In this sense, the order established by the disjunction prior--posterior presupposes the relationship of inequality and accordingly of plurality. Scotus asserts that either a being is prior or it is posterior, which amounts to the proposition that every being can be defined in terms of order.[26] Importantly, order is understood as a relationship of equivalence of that which is prior to that which is posterior and vice versa. This means that both the prior and the posterior are embedded in one common structure. Therefore, this order cannot be understood in such a manner that the prior, to which the posterior is related, establishes and constitutes this order while being exterior to this order.[27] Every being is ordered or related by the essence of what is a constituent element of the order. For this reason, two beings equal in relation to the whole order remain unequal one to another by their essence or quiddity. This leads Scotus to a distinction between the essential order of eminence, and the essential order of dependence.[28] For Scotus, such division is necessitated by the ambiguity of the very term "essential order", which is closely connected

[26] The order amounts to the relating of that which is posterior to that which is prior. It may have a characteristic of an essential order if something that is posterior remains in the necessary and not the contingent accidental relation to that which is prior. Underlying such necessity must then be the essence of the posterior; the relating is therefore, permanent. Comp. E.I. Zieliński, *op. cit.*, pp. 51–53.

[27] Comp. John Duns Scotus, *op. cit.*, chapter 1, p. 4. Scotus understands such order differently from Aristotle who assumed that everything that exists is relative to the Prime mover who himself is yet not relative to anything.

[28] John Duns Scotus, *op. cit.*, chapter 1, p. 4.

with the emergence of another pair of disjunctives. The order of eminence not only entails the existence of that which is prior but also implies that the prior exceeds in perfection. On the other hand, the posterior is that which is exceeded and dependent. Scotus states:

> [...] what is eminent is said to be prior whereas what is exceeded in perfection is posterior. Put briefly, whatever in essence is more perfect and noble would be prior in this manner.[29]

This entails that perfection with its gradation is the condition for all further classification, which must introduce the problem of a priori knowledge of that which is "pure perfection". We will turn to this issue later on when discussing "pure perfections"; here it is sufficient to say that perfection serves the gradation of individual beings within the order of guidditative being.[30]

In the order of dependence, the prior is that upon which something depends and the posterior is that which depends upon other thing for its existence. Scotus then boils down the relationship of dependence to the relationship of causality thereby introducing a new disjunction cause-caused. The disjunction is presented as an inequivalent relation in which the prior is a cause even if necessarily, it is the cause of that which is posterior (understood as a caused effect); consequently nothing could exist without a cause. In spite of this, as Scotus emphasizes, nothing indicates that the posterior demands the caused. Its existence is therefore entirely independent of the caused effect and in this sense it is prior. From the perspective of that which is posterior as a caused effect the matter looks entirely different inasmuch as the caused demands a prior cause for its existence; the existence of the caused effect without the existence of a cause would be an essential contradiction. Such an inequivalent relation encompasses the order of dependence. Scotus holds that every being which is posterior has to posses it, which is prior. This is subordination and with this reason one would maintain, that every being, which is posterior essential should be dependent from being, which is prior.[31]

In view of the foregoing, Scotus regards cause as essentially independent of any caused effect. Therefore, all created causes are essentially

[29] John Duns Scotus, *op. cit.*, chapter 1, p. 4.

[30] A.B. Wolter, *op. cit.*, p. 141.

[31] *Ibidem.*

contingent in relation to their caused effects within the framework of created being. For that reason it is crucial that we should distinguish between necessary and unnecessary causality; thus Scotus introduces primary and secondary causality. Both necessary and unnecessary causality can only be understood as relative, which consequently, leads Scotus to the rejection of Aristotle's standpoint whereby a cause is a cause regardless of the caused effect, in other words, it is a cause without the caused. Scotus argues that in spite of there existing a cause without a caused effect if something is a cause, then it will always be the cause relative to the caused effect.[32]

On such specific approach, Scotus posits dependence but also priority of a cause over its effect; hence, in the essential order, the existence of a cause and the caused effect is closely connected although, as mentioned earlier, a cause and the caused effect are inequivalent.[33] This leads to a further consequence that within the essential order of dependence, it is impossible for one and the same thing to be dependent upon itself, which entails that the essential order occurs only when it involves at least two things. This does not however make it impossible for one nature to be both the mover and that which is moved because between the mover and the being in motion there occurs no essential dependence but only accidental dependence. Scotus makes use of the classical Aristotelian doctrine of four causes (efficient, final, formal and material). The essential order can be expanded to all types of causes however, in the case of

---

[32] "Quanda ergo probatur secundum intentionem Aristotelis angelus non esse causatum, quia secundum ipsum est formaliter necessarium, dico quod ipse non posuit sita inter se repugnare causatum et formaliter necessarium, cum dicet Z Metaph. sempitemarum principia semper esse verissima necessa est, quia sunt aliis causa veritatis. Simpliciter ergo, quae ipse posuit formalitur concessit principia habere", *Quodlibetum* (further on quoted as Quodl.,) q. 7, n. 42 (II/1, 1262). An example of Scotus's polemic with Aristotle and his proponents may be the following passage: "Ad illud quod conditur de Philosophis, potest dici, quod multos contradictiones latentes concesserunt, sicut negaverunt communitur esse aliquod primum principium contingenter causans, sed contingentiam esse in entibus et aliqua contingenter fieri, sed contradictionem includit aliquid contingentur fieri in entibus, et primam causam necessario causare", Ord. II, d. 1, q. 3, n. 12 (III/1, 780). Comp. A.B. Wolter, *op. cit.*, p. 142.

[33] "Causa inquantum causa, prior sit natura causata inquantum causatum, et tamen causa inquantum causa est imul causata simulitate requisita ad correlativa", Ord. I, d. 2, p. 1, q. 3, n. 4 (III/1, 152–153).

the first two, we deal with a higher degree of perfection than in the case of material and formal causality. Consequently, in the latter case, the convertive disjunction only applies to some beings. This stems from the fact that both form and matter are only parts so they do not exist on their own outside the substantial structure; moreover, not all beings are formal and material in their internal structure. That is the reason why efficient and final causes lack imperfection. In this sense, every being may be related to the disjunction cause-caused if a cause is understood as efficient or final in the external reference. Efficient causality entails the existence of the caused, while final causality causes motion (by directing the caused onto the cause-agent).[34]

Scotus uses all the distinctions discussed so far to show the connotations of the fundamental disjunction of prior-posterior in terms of the essential order. This disjunction provides a simple and exhaustive division of being, thereby fulfilling the condition of full convertibility with being. Scotus points out that in the essential order, nothing can be related to itself but whenever we speak of some order, the order is relative, meaning that a thing is ordered to another thing, distinct from itself. For this reason, infinite regress, or *regressus ad infinitum,* is impossible in the essential order and consequently, ordering by essence must entail the existence of a first thing that cannot be further decomposed. The proposed disjunctions reflect the internal ordering in relation to the first thing and in that sense, they are the transcendental attributes of being as irreducibly simple (indecomposable) because they determine it fully and completely.

Studying the relationships between different essential orders indicates that if there exists an order of effective causality, then there must exist an order of final causality and an order of dependence; each of them pertains to one and the same being. Every being is thus ordered and it may be defined through order as follows:

[34] "Causalitas autem causae efficientis et conservantis non terminabatur nisi ad aliquod existere non increatum, quia nihil efficit se", Ord. III, d. 6, q. 1, n. 3 (III/2, 74–75). "This does not say that motion in so far as it is an accidental entity does not essentially depend on its respective cause. This, however, is another question", A.B. Wolter, *op. cit.*, p. 144.

> [...] not every being is poterior and not every being is prior, because in both case it should be accepted circulus in definiendo. So there is some being prior which is not posterior, therefore the first being and being posterior, whereas does not exist such being, which would not be either prior, nor posterior.[35]

In this line of argumentation, Scotus specifies the meaning of the primary disjunctions: prior-posterior, cause-effect and unconditioned-conditioned which fully exhaust being making it impossible for any being to exist as exterior to this order. There exists no being to which one may not refer either as prior or posterior, cause or caused, or which is either independent or dependent. This entails that these disjunctions may refer to being in its entirety – to being qua being which is the subject of metaphysics. Thus, they are the properties of metaphorically understood being as its internal transcendental determinations.

The remaining disjunctive attributes are fundamentally different from the above discussed. Although they are contradictorily opposed pairs, as attributes of being they are not coextensive with being. In other words, being need not necessarily divide into both members of disjunction but, following the law of disjunction, it must be contained in either of the members. The proposition that a being does not pertain to one disjunctive member is essential to state that it pertains to the other member. Thus both members are the opposite properties of being, yet not in the sense of opposition but contradiction.

Such approach leads to a fundamental problem of how to treat these members of disjunction with reference to being in the absolute dimension that is being neutral in relation to everything else. Does the possibility of being not to be subject to one member of disjunction add anything to it or not? In general, how to treat this absence; does it express any attribute of being or not? On the other hand, assigning being to one of the disjunctives should be regarded as adding to it new positive "beingness"; being neutral in itself, it does not require assigning one member of the alternative *either...or*, and therefore it becomes "exterior" to the very being. The

---

[35] John Duns Scotus, *op. cit.*, chapter 4, pp. 47–48.

member of disjunction thus loses the character of an internal attribute of being per se.

Such difficulties already emerge when analyzing the disjunction act-potency because it divides being, and there exists no being which is neither act or potency.[36] For Scotus the very notions of act and potency are ambiguous. He therefore begins with an analysis of their different meanings in order to determine in what sense the disjunction act-potency may be understood as a transcendental (transcategorial) attribute of being.

First, act and potency are seen as exact opposites of each other and as such, they pertain to every being. Following this line of thought, all being can be distinguished in terms of act and potency. On such approach however, act and potency may not be regarded as complimentary principia in the sense of an active and passive principle because they do not enter into a composite which would be whole. The reason is that if we regard potency as the opposite of act, then the potency may not form a whole composite with act as it is not derived from act. Consequently, act and potency do not enter into a composite like for instance form and matter with reference to physical being.

Assuming that the disjunction act-potency fully diversifies being and that whatever exists is actual through its cause, then also all absences are actual beings and so as entities, they must possess certain positiveness; thus they become the attributes of being.[37] Such proposition is questioned by Scotus who posits that act and potency cannot be treated as constituent elements of the composite of formal and material; as opposites they can however be actualized in one and the same physical being – since they pertain separately to form and matter. Here, we find reference to the

---

[36] "Hoc disiunctum convertit sicut potentia vel actus cum ente", QSMet. IV, q. 2, n. 10 (I, 143). The disjunction act-potency is very important for Scotus as it accounts for the differentiation of being in the context of the theory of the soul.

[37] Scotus justifies this as follows: "Si accipiatur actus, prout distinguitur contra potentiam secundum quae, scilicet actum et potentiam, totum ens dividitur, sic actus non convertitur cum forma. Secundum hoc enim, omne quod est extra causam suam, est in actu, et secundum hoc etiam privationes dicuntur esse actu, unde causas dicitur esse actualitur in oculo carente visci [...]. Si autem loquavis de actu, [...] secundum quod est actus respectus et actuans et distinguens, sic distinguitur contra receptivum, et materia est receptivum illo modo, et non est actus", Ord. II, d. 12, q. 2, n. 7 (III/1, 1078).

previously discussed issue of actuality of matter that is to say, its quality of having certain positive "beingness" independent and specific only to matter, while being simultaneously potential in relation to form. This potency is expressed in that matter remains dependent upon form (may be realized by form) and enters with form into the essential unity.[38] Another agreeable meaning of potency according to Scotus, is not treating it as an active or passive constituent of the composite or a total rejection of its logical meaning. However, in the case of the disjunctive relation of act and potency such proposition seems to be unacceptable for it requires the existence of both exact opposites.

In connection with the above, a question arises of how act and potency may be established as transcendental attributes of being. Firstly, Scotus emphasizes that if we want to regard act and potency as the properties primarily diversifying being, we must unconditionally relate them to the actual being. In other words, only being which is dependent upon its existence may be defined in terms of act and potency. It is only in the context of actual existence that actuality occurs, while potency is what relates the essence of being to the actual existence. Thus we call a being potential when it lacks actual existence. Existence expresses the actuality of that which is possible to come to existence and therefore, act and potency primarily diversify being but only within the order of being. So understood, act and potency are different from act and potency understood as essential (quidditative) or constituent elements of things. That which actually exists is being in act, whereas that which does not actually exist but is possible to exist is being in potency.[39]

Different conceptions of the relation act-potency discussed so far are contradictory to one another. If actual existence is never inherent in the essence of being (except God), then it cannot alter the very essence of

---

[38] "Et eadem modo aequivocatur de potentia, quia ut opponitur actui primo modo, dicut ens diminutem, cui scilicet non repugnat esse extra causam suam; ens autem in actu oppositum isti potentiae, est ens completum in suo esse extra causam suam, quodcumque sit illud. Alio modo potentia dicit principium receptiorum actus secundo modo dicti, sicut materia dicitur potentia et forma actus", Ord. IV, d. 11, q. 3, n. 11 (III/2, 709). Comp. A.B. Wolter, *op. cit.*, p. 146.

[39] It is related to Scotus's conceiving of being as that which does not exclude existence.

being in any way. This entails that on transcendental approach to act and potency, both the actual being and the logical aspect of potency must be taken into account. Such is the case when we treat being as possible through its essence to be actualized, or, in other words, to become an actually existing individual being. On this account, act and potency are of the same genus since for the potency to be the opposite of act, it is necessary to pertain to its actual existence – to that which is individual and specific. In that sense, being is first potential in relation to existence, and next it is actualized as individual. Potency is thereby revealed as certain imperfection, which may be improved by an act of existence. Thus appears the disjunction act-potency expressed within the essential order of dependence in which that which is initially potential in relation to existence later becomes something in act. Further analysis of the disjunction act-potency must be conducted within the essential order of perfection. Then, it is possible that if we treat it as the opposite of act, potency must be related to act not only by the same genus, but also by the same species, and finally, together with act, it will enter into numerical unity. Scotus presents his argument as follows:

> Potency and act not only exist in the same species, but also in area of the same numerical unity. [...] Individual as soon as is in act at present, before that it was in possibility.[40]

Therefore, it must be assumed that the disjunction act-potency fulfills the conditions of a transcendental attribute of being but only in the precise sense of the alternative "either...or". If we treat being as potential, then its opposite will be actual with actuality meaning actual existence provided that act and potency are of the same genus; otherwise, that which was previously potential could not later become actual, so it would not even be potential, as nothing can be potential relative to itself. On the other hand, act and potency also constitute numerical commonness since they pertain to one and the same individual owing to the fact that act improves something which initially was less perfect as potential.

[40] "Potentia et actus non sunt tantum eiusdem species, sed etiam inesdem numeri [...]. Illud enim individuum, quod nunc est in actu, illud idem fuit in potentia", Ord. II, d. 16, q. unica, n. 5 (III/1, 1107). Comp. A.B. Wolter, *op. cit.*, p. 148.

Deliberations on the disjunction act-potency are closely connected with the disjunction independent-dependent. The relation of dependence consists in that one being is conditioned by the other in such a manner that the first cannot exist without the other, whereas the latter can exist without the first. As understood by Scotus, the disjunction in terms of dependence pertains to every being since every being is either dependent or independent; the dependent is always defined in relation to the independent, at the same time the latter does not demand such reference by its essence. This does not entail that such being is independent in the absolute sense as its independence occurs in relation to that which is dependent.[41]

Scotus emphasizes that independence in this case signifies absence or negation of all attributes of the dependent; hence, independence must be expressed within the essential order in which everything is related to an absolutely first independent being. There is only one such independent being – i. e. *Primus*. Scotus focuses all his efforts of inference on proving the existence of such being because it will be *Primus* – first independent being, yet defined with reference to causality and perfection. Related to causality, there emerges purpose, hence each caused effect is directed onto its cause as purpose.

One can clearly see close links between different orders and consequently between different disjunctions relative one to another. A good example of this connection is what Scotus states about end and finality:

> One should not fail to mention a false opinion concerning the nature of the end, namely, that the final cause of a thing is its last operation or the object attained through this operation. If one were to think that this as such is the final cause, he would be wrong, because this follows the existence of the thing ordered to the end and the latter's existence is not essentially dependent upon it. But it is precisely that for the love of which the efficient cause brings something to be that, as loved, is the final cause of what was made, for it is to the beloved that the latter is ordered. At times, it may well be

[41] "Omne dependens dependet ad aliquid omnino et simplicitur independens, nunquam enim dependentia alicuius sufficienter terminatur, nisi ad aliquid omnino independens", Ord. I, d. 12, q. 1, n. 14 (III/1, 470).

> that the object of the ultimate operation is something loved in this way and therefore it would be the final cause. But it would not be because it is the term of such a nature's operation, but rather because it is loved by that which causes this nature.[42]

It emerges from this that the inference of the disjunction independent-dependent always boils down to establishing the kind of dependence within the essential order – and for this reason, it is regarded as causality, causation, purpose, etc. Only in this respect can we state that every being is either independent or dependent, which finally leads us to the existence of *Primus* – absolutely first independent being which is conceived of by Scotus in a specific way:

> The whole series of dependents then is dependent and upon something which is not one of the group,[43]

hence the conclusion:

> […] inasmuch as to be able to produce something does not imply any imperfection – a point evident from conclusion eight of chapter two – it follows that this ability can exist in some nature without imperfection. But if every cause depends upon some prior cause, then efficiency would never be found without imperfection. Consequently, an independent power to produce something can exist in some nature and this is simply first.[44]

Every imperfect being is thus ordered in the essential order of dependence in which there must exist one perfect being independent of every other element of this order. One can clearly see the premises leading Scotus to

---

[42] John Duns Scotus, *op. cit.*, chapter 2, pp. 12–13. A.B. Wolter comments: "Scotus shows that material and formal causality imply efficient and formal though not vice versa, and that wherever we have en effect of efficient causality the effect is also conditioned by a final cause. It is therefore finitum in the sense of being »finalised«. Hence his conclusion: »Quod omne finitum est excessum« […] implies that whatever is the result of any kind of causality is exceeded in perfection by some being", A.B. Wolter, *op. cit.*, p. 149, footnote 70.

[43] John Duns Scotus, *op. cit.*, chapter 3, p. 30.

[44] *Ibidem*, p. 31.

the proof for the existence of the first cause, the maximally excellent and fully independent being, which he infers from the disjunction independent--dependent. The disjunction is thus raised to a status of the transcendental attribute of metaphysical being since its alternative content points to the necessity of existence of a first cause within the essential order of what is naturally given. This necessity then leads Scotus to a pair of disjunctives that are opposed to one another: necessary-contingent. Further analysis must then concern the synthesis of the contingent and the necessary. In other words, necessity and contingence must be viewed as the transcendental attributes of being in the broadest sense – that is of being capable of becoming anything and as such, potential in the absolute sense. Therefore, Scotus first makes an attempt to explain the correlation between the notions of a necessary and contingent being in terms of logical possibility and impossibility.

Broadly speaking, logical possibility in view of metaphysics means the capacity of all being for existence. On this approach, every being which fulfills the conditions of being, that is to say, is a composite of properties constituting the entity, remains potential in relation to existence. On the other hand, impossibility will express the incapacity of being for existence and thus its not being an entity due to an internal contradiction. For this reason, a square circle may not exist because it is a contradiction in terms.

The capacity for existence is the most characteristic property of being as it does not exclude existence – *non repugnat esse*. Metaphysically speaking, incapacity is simply pure nothingness which merely has the status of a name or term. On these conclusions, Scotus states that necessity and contingency pertain to the capacity of being for existence and, in this sense, they are the internal properties of that which is potential. It is even more interesting as it demonstrates that Scotus probably[45] consid-

[45] For instance the suggestion of Wolter (*op. cit.*, p. 150). In footnote no. 72, we find an important remark: "Creatures insofar as they exist in the divine intellect as archetypal ideas are neither formally necessary or nor contingent, even though the act of the divine intellect by which they are produced in esse intellecto is necessary. Necessity and contingency, then apply to true existence (*esse simpliciter*) end not properly speaking to the esse secundum quid i.e. the esse intellectum".

ered necessity and contingency modes of existence having certain positive "beingness". According to Scotus, they never express absences but always pertain to some attributes. Therefore, in the absolute dimension, act and potency become the attributes of *being qua being* indicating the intrinsic unity of nature as essence with existence.[46]

If one attributes necessity to a being, then the necessity expresses the capacity of its essence and existence to form unity, which means precisely that such being may not be non-existent.[47] On the other hand, contingency is the absolute opposite of such state; it means that there is no unity between essence and existence. If such being came into existence, then the potency of its essence must have been realised. Necessarily, a cause was involved as being may not actualise its potency by itself, which leads us directly to causality; hence so close a relationship between the disjunction necessary-contingent and the principle of causality (disjunction cause-effect). Scotus holds that from the standpoint of causality, a contingent being is that which may have existence after not having it.[48] So understood, contingency requires a cause, which in the absolute dimension is the first cause – God; it is by God's will that the potential may become actual from non-existence and then possess the unity of essence and existence. This unity is the unity of so to speak two exterior "elements"; it is not a relationship of the two necessarily complementary members since essence is essence without existence, and the latter reaches it from the out-

[46] "Dico quod contingentia non est tantum privatio vel defectus entitatis [...]. Immo contingentia est modus positivus entitatis sicut necessitas est alius modus, et omne positivum, quod est in effectu, principalius est causa priore, et ideo non sicut deformitas est ipsius actus a causa secunda, et non causa prima, ita est contingentia, immo contingentia per prius est a causa prima quam secunda, propter quod nullum causatum esset formaliter contingens, nisi a causa prima contingentur causaret", Ord. I, d. 39, q. unica, n. 3 (III/1, 715).

[47] Necessity excludes all potency: "Necessitas autem simplicitur privat absolute possibilitatem huius oppositio", Ord. I, d. 39, q. unica, n. 3 (III/1, 715). At the same time, necessity also excludes causality, comp.: John Duns Scotus, *op. cit.*, chapter 3, fifth conclusion, pp. 34–35.

[48] "Some nature is contingent. It is possible for it to exist after being nonexistent, not of itself, however, or by reason of nothing, for in both these cases a being would exist by reason of what is not a being", John Duns Scotus, *op. cit.*, chapter 3, pp. 26–27.

side. Therefore, it is only when it is relative to existence that the essence is potential.[49]

For Scotus, the category of existence becomes the determinant of what is necessary and what is contingent. Necessity is expressed in the essence of being through its existence as a constituent element of its being "this" and none other. For this reason necessity always expresses certain perfection of what is potential and as such-imperfect. Contingency requires a cause of bringing into existence that which does not exist by its essence, that is to say, by necessity. As a result, necessity is a principle superior to contingency. However for necessity to come to be, there must be a possibility of combining the more perfect with the less perfect by virtue of the law of contradiction allowing for such a possibility. Consequently, the disjunction necessary-contingent is a pure alternative to "*either..., or...*" as one and the same element cannot be both necessary and contingent. It also is a transcendental attribute of being because its members do not express any deficiency but only a degree of perfection; it is higher for necessity and lower for contingency.

Another pair of disjunctives: infinite-finite is treated by Scotus in a specific way. Here disjunction pertains to being expressed quantitatively rather than qualitatively. Consequently, it will express quantitative perfection. Quantity is characteristic of all being; one can always ask the question "how many things are there?". Being may be defined through the two absolute dimensions of quantity as either finite or infinite. So precise a distinction cannot be drawn in terms of quality – it is difficult to express the quality of being through the attributes of finitude or infinity. Indicating quality is rather an attempt at answering the question of what kind of being we are dealing with.[50] However, this refers to being

---

[49] A.B. Wolter, *op. cit.*, p. 151.

[50] "Finitum tamen et infinitum non dividunt ens, nisi ens quantum, quia sicut [...] finitum et infinitum quantitati congruunt, quod est verum de finito et infinito, et quantitate proprie acceptis, ita etiam extensive loquendo, finitum et infinitum, ut sunt passiones entis, conveniunt praecise enti quanta in se habenti quantitatem aliquiam perfectionem; talis autem quantitas non convenit entitati, nisi quae potest esse partialis vel totalis inter essentias", Quodl., q. 5, n. 25 (II/1, 1220).

in terms of its scope; that is to say, the actual being we are dealing with in reality.

Scotus tries to extend the notion of quantity by pointing to its virtual nature. It then appears to be the magnitude or power which may serve as the basis for determining all transcendental dependence. Scotus holds that with reference to magnitude, we can establish whether a being is big or small, or, whether it is equal or unequal. In the most adequate sense this founding of everything in magnitude goes with God, which is why in this case size exists without quantity, because any quantitative reference is already founded in this biggest and absolute size. Thus magnitude cannot be classified quantitatively.[51] Here Scotus makes use of a distinction proposed by Saint Augustine who, in the treatise *On the Holy Trinity*, defined magnitude as the "enormousness of power" rather than something measurable in terms of quantity. So understood, magnitude situates itself above any specific quantity and explicitly shows the virtual nature of quantity.[52] Quantity-magnitude, so understood, pertains to all being. Firstly, Scotus assumes that every being is something in itself, and as such, it possesses essence and what is more, it has in itself a certain degree of determination which situates it in relation to other beings. Briefly, a being in itself is determined – bound to a place it holds in the order of being.[53] This ordering will then reflect the magnitude of its excellence, in other words: the more perfect a being is, the higher it is situated in the ontological hierarchy. Furthermore, the magnitude of excellence is expressed in two modes: as either limited or unlimited. If a being exhibits

[51] "Dico quod non est ibi [sc. in Deo] quantitas malis, sed virtutis, [...] tunc potest proprie concedi, quod est magnitudo ibi sine quantitate, et ita magnitudo vere est fundamentum aequalitatis transcendentis, quia hoc modo omne ens est magnum vel parvum, aequaele vel inaequele, licet magnitudo ista non fit fundamentum aequalitatis, prout est passio quantitatis, quae est genus", Quodl., q. 5, n. 25 (II/1, 1220).

[52] "Et secundam haec sicut potest considerari quodcumque ens, ita etiam super ipsum potest fundari triplex relatio communitur sumpta, quia identitus super quodcumque ens inquantum est quid, et aequalitas vel inaequalitas super quodcumque ens, inquantum habet magnitudinem aliquam perfectionis quae dicitur quantitas virtutis", Ord. I, d. 19, q. 1, n. 3 (III/1, 548).

[53] "Dico quod quodcumque ens est in se quid et habet in se aliquem quadum determinatum in entibus", Ord. I, d. 19, q. 1, n. 3 (III/1, 548).

limited magnitude, then it is finite and if it exhibits unlimited magnitude, then it is infinite.[54]

Thus the decisive determinant of the finitude or infinity of being is for Scotus its limitation or limitlessness. The oppositional character of this pair is determined through pointing out that all being is always finite in quidditative terms since the quiddity never expresses anything else but the boundaries within which a thing is "the thing" (has *quid*). Scotus emphasizes that in this sense what is not limited is unlimited and thereby infinite.[55]

Finitude and infinity play a crucial role in Scotus's metaphysics and its relation to theology (understood as *theologia pro nobis*). For him the two exemplify the so-called "intrinsic ways of existing" and in this regard, they are quidditative presentations of being without considering the order of being.[56] In his deliberations on the disjunction infinite-finite, Scotus eventually leaves aside the actual excellence of that which exists. Consequently, he acknowledges all excellence in God – as an infinite being, to be formally infinte.[57] In that lies the absolute dimension of God's magnitude.

---

[54] "Infinitis in entitute dicit totalitatem in enititate, et per oppositum suo modo finites dicit partialitatem entitatis. Omne enim finitum ut tale, minus est infinito ut tale", Quodl., q. 5, n. 4 (II/1, 1207–1208). Comp. A.B. Wolter, *op. cit.*, p. 154.

[55] "Quidquid dicitur communiter de Deo et creatura, est indifferens ad finitum et infinitum (loquendo de essentialibus), vel saltem ad finitum et non finitum (loquendo de quibuscumque), quia relatio divina, nec est finita, nec infinita; nullam autem genus potest esse indifferens ad finitum et infinitum [...]. Quidquid est in Deo perfectio essentialis et formaliter infinitum, in creatura vero finitum", Ord. I, d. 8, p. 1, q. 3, n. 16 (III/1, 394). Scotus relates finitude and infinity to the relationship between creatures and God. It is only God who is an infinite being; this is inferred from His not being limited in any way. The question concerns the cognizability of God – an infinite being and constructing by Scotus a theology which is knowledge – a science possible for a human.

[56] "Infinitas est magis modus intrinsecus essentiae quam aliquod atributum", Quodl., q. 5, n. 5 (II/1, 1208–1209).

[57] "Omnis autem realitas in Deo est infinita formalitur", Ord. I, d. 8, p. 1, q. 3, n. 25 (III/1, 402). It is worth emphasizing that Scotus understands reality – *realitas* – as formal excellence. With reference to this, A.B. Wolter writes the following: "The entitias hypostatica is not a perfection in the proper sense of the term, otherwise each of the Divine Persons would be imperfect because he lacked the precise formal personality of the others", A.B. Wolter, *op. cit.*, pp. 154–155, footnote 93. Such formal conception of perfection in God as First Principle entails the following propositions. Second coclusion: "Whatever is intrinsic to the supreme nature is such in the highest degree"; Third conclusion:

All this is significant when studying the qudditative order of perfections since it is ultimately contained in what is finite and leads to what is infinite. Pursuing dependence, it is possible to finally reach an absolutely primary division into the finite and the infinite[58]. In this sense, the disjunction infinite-finite fulfills the fundamental condition of an internal property of being unconditionally dividing it (determining it) into infinite and finite beings, simultaneously leading us to acknowledge the existence of a first being in the order of dependence.[59] This however, requires further division.

Directly connected to the disjunction infinite-finite is another disjunction, that of absolute-relative. Scotus deals with it when he is concerned with the problem of the Trinity; for instance a following question arises:

> Whether Divine Persons are constituted in Their personal existences through original relationships or through else something absolute?[60]

Undoubtedly, for Scotus the disjunction absolute-relative is of transcendental nature as it is coexistent with being of God in the broadest metaphysical sense. It is different with reference to a particular physical being or a thing because it is impossible that both the absolute and relative, as opposites, pertain to one and the same object. Nevertheless, as formally opposed they form a different relation with any other relation although in reality, this relation may turn out to be identical with the very basis.[61] Any

---

"Every pure perfection is predicated of the supreme nature as being present necessarily and in the highest degree", John Duns Scotus, *op. cit.*, chapter 4, p. 52.

[58] Comp. the six proofs of the infinity of being of God in *A Treatise on God as First Principle* (*ibidem*, pp. 69–92).

[59] Scotus writes the following: "Unum infinitum sufficientur terminat dependentiam omnium finitorum, et specialitur primum a quo dependent", Quodl., q. 5, n. 9 (II/1, 1210).

[60] "Utrum personae divinae constituantur in esse personali per relationes originis vel per aliquia absoluta?", Ord. I, d. 26, q. unica (III/1, 699). The problem in a similar context is discussed by Saint Bonaventure in *On the Mystery of the Holy Trinity* (see s. Bonaventure, *op. cit.*, pp. 139–274).

[61] "Proprietas ut proprietas est aliqua entitas, alioquin non constitueret aliquod ens, aut igitur entitas ad se, aut ad altrum, aut neutrum. Entitatem enim aliquam esse singularem, quae nec sit entitis ad se nec ad aliud, non videtur esse intelligibile; ergo oportet quod ista entitas formalitur, vel sit ad se et tunc constituit personam absolutam, vel ad alteram, et tunc ut proprietas est relatio", Ord. I, d. 28, q. 3, n. 2 (III/1, 644).

relation leads then to the choice of something absolute that is founded in the very nature of the relation. This comes from the fact that any relation assumes the presence of two interrelated elements, which brings about the necessity of providing an absolute basis for the relation. It is then from this point of view that Scotus claims that both the basis-foundation of the relation and the elements of the relation must be eventually treated as absolute. This is because the foundation cannot include the relation of which it is the basis since in that case it would not be a relation in respect of something else (which is the essence of the sense of the relation between two distinct elements) but in relation to itself. Apart from that, foundation cannot be a member of the relation of which it is the basis. For this reason, there exists a difference between the basis and the elements of the relation such that they are absolute, that is, they are different but closely related. According to Scotus this can be well seen in the case of trinitary relation, which exemplifies the maximal identity of its foundation (basis) and an absolute difference in each of the parts of the relation.[62]

The essential relation holds between two extremities, each of which is indispensable for the relation. The destruction of any extremity leads to the destruction of the relation. In this sense they are indispensable but

[62] "Fundamentum ergo relationis est aliqua entitas formalitur non includens illam relationem formaliter, quia si formaliter includeret eam, non esset formaliter relatio ad iliud, sed ad se, quia fundamentum suum est formalitur ad se, cum quo ponitur formalitur idem. Nec posset esse fundamentum primum relationis ad hoc enim esset quaerere de illa relatione prima in qua ponevetur, non est ergo praecise aliqua relatio fundamentum alicuius relationis quod etiam apparet in relationibus divinis, ubi est maxima identitas in fundamento, et tamen fundamentum non est formaliter relatio", Ord. I, d. 26, q. unica, n. 12 (III/1, 602). Comp. Rep. I, d. 13, q. unica, n. 10 (II/2, 201). Scotus's understanding of relation and its foundation corresponds to the assumptions of Saint Bonaventure in the context of his deliberations on the Holy Trinity. Bonaventure writes the following among other things: "Dicendum, quod respectivum est duplex: quoddam, quod dicit respectum ad aliud diversum secundum essentiam; quoddam, quod non dicit respectum nisi ad aliquid silii consubstantiale. Primo modo respectivum includit quondam dependentiam, ac per hoc et defectum dicit a simplicitate summa; secundo modo non dicit aliquam dependentiam nec defectum a simplicitate summa, maxime quando ipsum suppositum est sua proprietas, qua refertur; et hoc modo ponitur respectus in proprietatibus divinarum personarum, non primo modo, et ita nulla ex hoc introducitur compositum", s. Bonaventura, *op. cit.*, q. 3, a. 2, p. 77.

they are dependent on each other, that is relative in terms of real reference, which is why the relation in its foundation must refer to the real. This allows Scotus to claim that the destruction of a real relation brings forth not only the elimination of the relation but also of its basis and foundation.[63] The relation of relativity seems to be a kind of form whereas foundation and terms (members or extremities) seem to be a kind of matter. Under such understanding, the nature of the relationship between all elements of a relation, i.e. the very relation, the basis and extremities is not entailed by the causal ordering. Thus it is not a necessary relationship or a result of an act. In this sense the disjunction absolute-relative refers to a being – subject to the disjunction, where every being is either absolute or relative – relational.

The next disjunction substance-accident poses a problem when defined as transcendental since both substance and accident belong to the categorial order and not the transcategorial one. Scotus makes it clear however that substance, especially when assigned to God, can be conceived of also in another way. In this case substance is not subject to any limitations and consequently it cannot be expressed categorially but it expresses a being for itself and not a being in terms of anything else. This understanding of substance is abstracted from any limited being (finite and infinite), and it is precisely this understanding that is more common than the concept of substance as genus (i.e. treated categorially).[64] A crucial element of Scotus's philosophy is that he accepts such a broad understanding of substance through the prism of substance excluding any boundness by something else, thus always remaining autonomous and independent. By contrast, accident is always *bounded by something else*, which can be considered the most general manifestation of its nature. In this sense

[63] "Respectus est essentialiter habitudo inter duo extrema, et ideo sicut tollere terminum ad quem est respectus est tollere vel destruere respectum, ita tollere illud cuius est respectus, est tollere respectum est destruere rationem respectus", Ord. IV, d. 12, q. 1, n. 8 (III/2, 755).

[64] "Si substantiam abstrahus a creata et increata, non accipitur ibi substantia ut est conceptus generis generalissimi, quia increata repugnat substantia hoc modo quia substantia hoc modo includit limitationem, sed accipitur ibi substantia pro ente in se, et non ente in alio, cuius conceptus prior est, communior conceptu substantiae ut est genus", Ord. I, d. 8, p. 1, q. 3, n. 25 (III/1, 402). Comp. A.B. Wolter, *op. cit.*, p. 152.

accident can be treated supracategorially as nature pertaining to any concrete accident.[65] In this way substance and accident exhaust the being in its totality as any being is either (unbound) substance or (bound) accident. In consequence we deal here with a transcendental disjunction that represents being in the order of existence and not essence. In the latter case it would be tantamount to representing substance and accident as traditional categories.

The remaining disjunctions proposed by Scotus can be treated together. One of them is the disjunction simple-complex. Simple being is the one without any parts whereas complex being has interrelated parts that form a unity.[66] The unity of each composite results from the actual potential relation to which any composite is subject. Thus it is in terms of act and potency that the structure of complex being be understood.[67] What follows is that parts of the composite remain in the relation act-potency and that the very composite can be treated as actual and potential. The actual composite is excellence per se, yet not absolute excellence. This stems from the fact that the range of each composite includes the aspect of potential as what is an actually existing composite must have become it after being only potential. Consequently, the relation is considered in a broader context of relations, which points to the absence of full and absolute excellence in the composite. What can be found in the order of dependence is the relation between the simple and the complex. That is why in relation to being it can be accepted that the disjunction simple-complex refers to it as a transcendental attribute. It should be remembered though that Scotus did not discuss the problem extensively.[68]

---

[65] See Quodl., q. 3, n. 19 (II/1, 1186–1187).

[66] "Quia compositum non est illud quod est nisi ex partibus en hoc non ut divisis, sed ut unitis, ut patet ex VII Metaphysicae [cap. 17] respectu huius syllabae ab, de a et b, ita universaliter de partibus et toto", Quodl., q. 9, n. 8 (II/1, 1281). Comp. John Duns Scotus *op. cit.*, chapter 4, p. 102.

[67] "Dico quod compositio potest intelligi proprie prout est ex re actuali et re potentiali vel minus proprie, prout est exrealitate et realitate actuali et potentiali in eadem re", Ord. II, d. 3, p. 1, q. 6, n. 16 (III/1, 931).

[68] An interesting issue, which Scotus only mentions, is expressing the relation simple-complex in another order of dependence which would point to the dependence between that which is made from parts and its parts. See A.B. Wolter, *op. cit.*, pp. 157–158.

As the remaining disjunctives proposed by Scotus did not enjoy much discussion either, I shall only list them here: one-many,[69] similar-different,[70] related to the disjunction equal-unequal quantitatively, which in turn leads to the disjunctive big-small also understood quantitatively.[71]

To sum up, the presented list of disjunctives as transcendental (trans-categorial) attributes of being is not exhaustive but rather than provide a closed and complete list Duns Scotus intends to show the universal law of disjunction operating as what constitutively and fundamentally belongs to being understood in its broadest metaphysical sense. Disjunctives make it possible to build the metaphysical structure since by pointing to the internal properties of being, they set to what is absolutely common boundaries marking the diversity of being. Under such a definition the role of disjunctives is fundamental because thanks to them it is possible to discriminate being, that is to say, to indicate its attributes and manifestations starting from its highest representation of being as being to more and more specific ones. By means of disjunction Scotus demonstrates the primary transcendental structure of being. At the same time disjunctives as contraries divide being and thus show the perfect and the imperfect. Undoubtedly, disjunctives are positive properties. Even though they are mutually exclusive (contradictions), they do not lack anything. Scotus emphasizes that they are contradictions but they must exist positively as they function as intrinsic determinants and being properties they cannot express deficiencies. The following extract can serve as a fine example of Scotus's intuition:

[69] "Unum et multa sunt opposita immediante dividentia ens [...] quae circa quodcumque includunt contradictionem, et non unum in ente est multa necessario", QSMet. I, q. 1, n. 23 (I, 16–17).

[70] "Dicit Philosophus 1. Metaph. quod 'Omne ens omni enti componatum, est idem vel diversum, ita quod omne ens omni enti eam partum est aequale vel inaequale. Sicut igitur fundamentum identitatis, aequalitatis est similitudinis hoc modo communitur sumptum, est ens in communi comparatum ad quodcumque ens in communi, ita et illae relationes sunt transcendenes, licet non convertibiles, cum disjunctione tamen dividentes ens, sicut dividitur in necessarium et possibile", Ord. I, d. 19, q. 1, n. 3 (III/1, 548).

[71] "Aequale et inaequale non dicantur nisi secundum quantitatem. Quantitas aliquo modo convenit omni enti cuiuscumque generis, et per consequans licet magnum et parvum secundum eum sint passiones propriare quantitatis, tamen translative accepta sunt transcendentia, et passiones totius entis", Quodl., q. 6, n. 5 (II/1, 1223). Comp. A.B. Wolter, *op. cit.*, s. 158.

"White man" and "Non-white man" are not opposites, yet in relation to man [being] white and [being] non-white are mutually exclusive contradictions. In the same way "being in subject" and "not being in subject" are mutually exclusive contradictions. Scotus treats disjunctives as positive properties transcending the structure of categories, which serve as the basis for natural knowledge available to intellect and reaching the cognition of true being of God.[72]

[72] Scotus writes the following: "You are truly what it means to be, you are the whole of what it means to exist. This, if it be possible for me, I should like to know by way of demonstration. Help me then, O Lord, as I investigate how much our natural reason can learn about that true being which you are if we begin with the being which you have predicated of yourself", John Duns Scotus, *op. cit.*, chapter 1, p. 3.

9 788378 501466

www.ingramcontent.com/pod-product-compliance
Ingram Content Group UK Ltd.
Pitfield, Milton Keynes, MK11 3LW, UK
UKHW021823190726
13853UKWH00003B/1160

9 788378 501466